Praying
AS LIVING REMINDERS

⸺∞⸺

*Morning and Evening Prayer
with Henri Nouwen*

DAVID HAAS

clear *faith*
PUBLISHING

Gospel Canticle for Morning Prayer
Luke 1: 68-79 (DH, adapt.)
The Canticle of Zachary (Benedictus)

God be blessed!
I am now free, because I belong to God.
God is coming, over and over again,
> to raise me up,
> to open my eyes,
> to dwell in my heart,
> to rescue my life.

The voices of friends and messengers
> have entered into my space;
> they are sent every day,
> sharing and announcing to me the amazing
> truth
> that all that is evil, in the end, will not win;
> that hate cannot and will not poison and infect
> the wonderful and good that is in me—
> in all of us.

Mercy abounds!
Promises kept!
Covenant sealed!
I once was imprisoned by darkness,
> And I am now filled with light.
I was once paralyzed and unable to praise;
> now my doors of joy fling open without fear.
I, all of us, are holy, beloved;
> vessels of justice in God's eyes.
> Always.

I am the beloved;
> I am an ambassador,
> a witness to this most holy presence.

I must announce, prepare,
and have my eyes, ears and heart be opened
to continually and humbly receive the story
of how God is loving,
of how God is saving,
of how God forgives all of us,
over and over again.

Tenderness.
Compassion.
These are my names for God,
who dawns from the highest place,
shining through,
shattering the dark,
protecting me in my deepest corners,
loosening the stranglehold of hate,
and the horror and fear of death.

For God decides,
and will always choose
to guide my way,
and forever lead me
to a deep and lasting peace.

(Lk 1:68-79/Excerpt from *Welcome, Faithful Presence*)

Praying
AS LIVING REMINDERS

―∞∞∞―

*Morning and Evening Prayer
with Henri Nouwen*

DAVID HAAS

Published by Clear Faith Publishing, LLC
22 Lafayette Road
Princeton, NJ 08540
www.clearfaithpublishing.com

Cover artwork: *Out of the Dark* © Jan Richardson. janrichardson.com

Back cover photo of David Haas: Sharie Bowman

Cover Design by Doug Cordes
Interior Design by Doug Cordes

ISBN 978-1-940414-17-1

ALSO BY DAVID HAAS
AVAILABLE FROM CLEAR FAITH PUBLISHING

(www.clearfaithpublishing.com)

Welcome, Faithful Presence:
A Week of Praying the Hours with Henri Nouwen

(Paperback edition and 3-CD audio book)

Blessed are the Merciful:
Stations to Celebrate the Way of God's Mercy

(Available in paperback edition and Assembly edition)

Walk with Christ:
Celebrating the Way of the Nativity,
the Cross, and the Resurrection

(Paperback edition)

My Heart Is Ready:
Psalm-Poems for Prayer & Proclamation

(Paperback edition)

Praying and Singing as the Beloved of God

(Digital download)

To Stephen Pishner

My friend and brother in the Lord

Contents

Foreword xiii

Introduction xvii

Morning & Evening Prayer 1

      Week One. 3

      Week Two 55

      Week Three 109

      Week Four 159

Psalm-Poems for Midday Prayer 213

Psalm-Poems for Night Prayer 223

Invitatories, Antiphons, & Canticles 235

Musical Suggestions 279

Seasonal Reflections 291

Blessings & Other Prayers. .299

Indexes 307

Gratitude 311

Sources 315

About the Author 320

Foreword

David Haas is a man of passion, wisdom, and artistry. David grasps the wholeness of being: the oneness of body and spirit, the singer and the song, the secular and the sacred. As a person of deep faith, he has, through his many musical compositions and his writings, revealed himself as a person of his time: one who searches, ponders, adapts and celebrates.

Over the years, I have observed David's transition from musical composition to the unfolding and gushing forth of poetry and ponderings. From him, I have heard the utterances of a human heart, the thoughts of an active mind, and the determination to live life fully. The title of this new book, *Praying as Living Reminders*, complements the invitation to holiness that has been known to so many in his music. His "Blest Are They" now becomes "Living Reminders." We are to be reminders of divine love and mercy so beautifully expressed in the psalms of long ago.

In the psalms, David finds an "entire galaxy of the human condition addressed and celebrated: joy, peace, contentment, solace, praise, gratitude, and thanksgiving—as well as the laments of sadness, loneliness, anger, pain and suffering, disillusionment, and rage." (See "Introduction," page xvii.) Each of us, at some time or another, has lived those emotions. In adapting the psalms, I sense that David is sharing his own vulnerability. He reminds us, as Paul does, that "when I am weak, then I am strong" (2 Corinthians 12:10). In these pages, we find an invitation to be vulnerable, to be open to grace, to hear the gentle voice of the divine from within and without. There is a synergy in the psalms that takes one beyond the words and images to a place called *Source*, where the freshness of inspiration flows in abundance.

David was, as he says in his introduction, reenergized by the call for renewal at the Second Vatican Council. His book responds to the call to universal holiness by offering a pattern of prayer for the entire People of God: highlighting the morning and evening times to praise, to be silent, and to be motivated is greatly enriched by the truth, beauty, and joy of the psalms and canticles.

This current work of the Psalter and the reminders of Henri Nouwen serves as a bridge between the teachings of the Hebrew times and the modern day saints. Henri is, most definitely, one of the cloud of contemporary witnesses.

We live in challenging, chaotic times. We live in magnificent and mystical times! Our world is searching for love, for meaning and wisdom. The scientific community asserts that the universe is expanding. Isn't it a mystery of how we, too, are evolving, moving into the beyond? The universe models to us the joy and chaos of change. An expanding universe is an image for us...to penetrate the depths of who we are and our home in the universe. We can clearly see, in examples like Psalm 139 and Psalm 8, that it is so clear that we have been in God all this time!

In Henri, David met a soul mate. David says that Henri's entire life ached to discover how the spiritual life could be accessed and celebrated in fresh and vibrant ways. Like him, David wants to integrate the beauty of the psalms and its author and psalmist into a rhythm of contemporary times. Both Henri and David were and are driven by the desire to penetrate the secular with the Good News. Again, the title of this mystical book, *Praying as Living Reminders*, is in itself a meditation. It is a call for all of us to be living reminders of our own magnificence in God's eyes—to be witnesses to the world of who we are meant to be: people who praise God, who cannot help themselves in being anything but totally engaged in the mission to energize and make holy our beloved sisters and brothers. Using the Word of God and Henri's words, we are invited to act justly, love tenderly, and walk humbly with our God.

Praying as Living Reminders is user-friendly. There is a freedom in the organization that invites, rather than imposes, form and matter. Its sources include a comprehensive index, music, seasonal prayers, and blessings. Readers ("pray-ers") will rejoice in the inclusiveness of language but also in its ecumenical outlook. This well-organized book of prayer invites us to pause, to listen, and to sing our busy lives into a dance. Some may say that this book is for a new generation, the "today "generation. Henri reminds us that such prayer is radical because it invites us to lay down our old selves and to accept our new self, which is Christ. Perhaps this book is best described as a daily prayer-filled celebration that will help make all things new— through, with, and in this very Christ.

Pearl Gervais,
a friend and companion on the journey

Introduction

Our demon says:
"We are too busy to pray;
we have too many needs to attend to,
too many people to respond to,
too many wounds to heal.
Prayer is a luxury,
something to do during a free hour,
a day away from work or on a retreat.
The few who are exclusively concerned with
prayer—
such as Trappists, Poor Clares,
and some isolated hermits—
are really not involved with ministry.
They are set free for single-minded contemplation
and leave Christian service to others."
But to think this way is harmful;
harmful for ministers as well as for contemplatives.
Service and prayer can never be separated...

(Henri Nouwen, *The Living Reminder: Service and Prayer
in the Memory of Jesus Christ*)

Throughout my life as an adult Christian and servant minister, there have always been three key sources that have anchored my prayer life and spirituality: my love of the psalms; my equal passion for the prayer of the Church, The Liturgy of the Hours; and the gift and source of wisdom that explodes forth from the writings and teachings of Henri Nouwen.

The Psalter provides lovers of scripture with what could arguably be seen as the most "human" and vulnerable book of the entire Bible. In these ancient prayer-poems, we find the entire galaxy of the human condition addressed and celebrated: joy, peace, contentment, solace, praise, gratitude, and thanksgiving—as well as the laments of sadness, loneliness, anger, pain and suffering, disillusionment, and rage. These utterances of the human heart are timeless, which is why they continue to serve the prayer life of Jews and Christians—and other spiritual seekers—to this very day.

The Liturgy of the Hours is the ritual celebration of the call to "pray without ceasing" (1 Thessalonians 5:17) that has been with us throughout our Christian history. It was reenergized by the request for its renewal at the Second Vatican Council as a pattern of prayer not only for priests and religious, but for the entire people of God, the Body of Christ. The appeal of this spiritual marking of time and keeping the hours of the day holy (morning, midday, evening, and night) led to one of the reforms of the Council in providing a four-week cycle (especially for morning and evening prayer) to serve as a path for those who had previously found it difficult to sink into.

And then, there is Henri. Henri was a priest from the Netherlands whose entire life was an ache to discover how the spiritual life could be accessed and celebrated in fresh and vibrant ways. He taught at many renowned universities in his home country and, in the United States, at Notre Dame, Yale, and Harvard. But Henri's search to deepen the journey of holiness led him to many other journeys, which included the Trappist Abbey of the Genesee in upstate New York; to Latin America, and in particular, Peru; and lastly, to his final home and destination serving as pastor for the L'Arche Daybreak Community in Toronto, Canada, until his death in 1996.

Henri is thought by many to be the most significant spiritual writer since Thomas Merton, and his many books on the spiritual life include such classics as *The Wounded Healer*, *Creative Ministry*, *Life of the Beloved*, *The Return of the Prodigal Son*, *Here and Now*, and *The Inner Voice of Love*. His amazing gift to present the spiritual life in a simple, direct, and yet profound way has infused the spiritual DNA of thousands and thousands over the years, those seeking to grow closer to God, to themselves, and to all sisters and brothers who are making a similar journey. I believe that Henri's writings are most authentically a living scripture for us in our present age, just as the gospels and other writings of the New Testament were for the early Christian community. His wisdom speaks and teaches what we, as a contemporary "Church," need to embrace as followers of Christ.

Henri tirelessly taught and lived the relationship between prayer and solitude and how it is tethered to the call to discipleship and action. Ministry and spirituality cannot, and must not, be separated. One of his marvelous images for those in ministerial leadership is that we are all called to be "living reminders" of Jesus Christ. (This is developed more fully in his book, *The Living Reminder: Service and Prayer in Memory of Jesus Christ*.) Our service and prayer is a means of more deeply announcing the presence of Jesus in our lives and of seeing our vocation to be "witnesses of God's love" as the "beloved."

Again, from Henri's *The Living Reminder*:

First, as a healing reminder,
second as a sustaining reminder,
third as a guiding reminder.

If we are to serve and be such witnesses of God's love as healing, sustaining, and guiding reminders, our formation to such a cause must be centered in the discipline and focus of breathing in Christ, in the unceasing life of prayer. This is the center of this prayer resource that you now hold in your hands. *Praying as Living Reminders* is an adaptation of the four-week morning and evening cycle of prayer. Instead of being laced with passages from the canonical Hebrew and New Testament scriptures, Henri's wisdom is presented here as a proclamation of God's "Word," meaning, a revelation of the Holy Presence of God in our midst. As we journey throughout the day, Henri's enlightened words can speak to us and help us in the hourly journey to be the "living reminders" of Jesus Christ that we are called to be.

My first book honoring the fusion of daily prayer and Henri's spirituality, *Welcome, Faithful Presence: A Week of Praying the Hours with Henri Nouwen* (also published by Clear Faith Publishing) was an initial exploration of how his wisdom could be "prayed" as well as read. The book's popularity in both paperback and audio provoked in me an invitation to deepen that journey with this resource.

This ecumenical version of Morning and Evening Prayer utilizes a short form of the two "hinges" of the Liturgy of the Hours, Morning Prayer and Evening Prayer. Also provided here are "poetic" adaptations of psalms and reflections by Henri that are appropriate for Midday Prayer, Night Prayer, and for Table Blessings.

The prayer patterns offered in these pages are intended for individuals as well as for smaller groups of people who gather in parishes and households for meetings, as well as in settings such as retreats, parish missions, and other gatherings for spiritual renewal.

The form of this four-week cycle of Morning and Evening Prayer is very simple:

- *Invitatory / The Sign of the Cross*
  This is an introductory verse. Those praying can either use or adapt the invitatories provided on pages 235–278 or can insert their own.

- *Optional Song or Hymn*
  Suggestions for these are offered on pages 270–290.

- *Two Psalms*
  Adapted here as "Psalm-Poems," these are separated by a short pause for silent prayer.

- *From Henri*
  A short, reflective passage from the wisdom of Henri Nouwen.

- *Silent Reflection*
  A brief pause for silent reflection.

- *Gospel Canticle*
  The Canticle of Zachary/ Benedictus for Morning Prayer and *The Canticle of Mary/Magnificat* for Evening Prayer are found on the front and back inside covers.

- *Prayers of Gratitude (Morning) and Intercession (Evening)*

- *The Lord's Prayer*

- *Sharing of the Peace / The Sign of the Cross*
  These are accompanied by a plea for blessing.

With only a few exceptions, the psalms—or as I call my contemporary adaptions of these holy texts, "Psalm-Poems"—come from the psalms that are appointed for the Liturgy of the Hours. Additional canticles from the Hebrew Scriptures and the New Testament may also be added, and those poetic adaptations can be found on pages 235–278.

The chosen sections from Henri Nouwen's writing are seen here as the "scripture," one could say, for the time of prayer. That being the case, no other passages from scripture are appointed except for the "psalm-poems" and canticles.

Regardless of whether these times of prayer are prayed alone or in group settings, the pace of the prayer should be peaceful, focused, and attentive. It is better to keep things simple than to just hurry and race through the different elements of the prayer. One option to consider is that the Evening Prayer could be used as a time of prayer before or after the praying of the dinner meal—or said in parts throughout the stages of the meal.

When groups are praying together, it is suggested that different people take parts, such as one or two different people to read and pray the "psalm-poems" and the canticle, and another to read the reflection of Henri Nouwen. The lighting of a candle can be a good central symbol for all to gather around for the time of prayer.

If we really want to take on the call to be living memories, witnesses of God's love who constantly renew ourselves in all things new in our lives of prayer and service, our cause has to be one led by surrendering ourselves to God—to move downward from our minds to the center of our hearts. Disciplines of prayer, such as what is offered here, can help us discover that. Immersing ourselves in the human journey of the psalms, which some call the daily "murmuring" of our total reliance upon God, can help us revel in and celebrate our sense of being beloved by God. And Henri's lens of the Spirit that moves and stirs and breathes in us can provide a new source of wisdom for the journey "through, with, and in" the blessed and most present—Christ, yesterday, today, and forever—throughout all time.

David Haas
April 25, 2017
The Feast of St. Mark

Morning & Evening Prayer

God is not someone who was or will be,
but the One who is,
and who is for me in the present moment.

(HN, *Here and Now: Living in the Spirit*)

WEEK ONE

Often I have said to people,
"I will pray for you,"
but how often did I really enter into the full reality
of what that means?
I now see how indeed I can enter deeply
into the other and pray to God from his center.
When I really bring my friends
and the many I pray for
into my innermost being
and feel their pains,
their struggles,
their cries in my own soul,
then I leave myself, so to speak,
and become them,
then I have compassion.

(HN, *The Genesee Diary*)

Sunday Evening Prayer I

Invitatory / The Sign of the Cross

Optional Song or Hymn

Psalm 141:1–5, 8–10

> *Help my prayers rise to you like burning incense.*
> *My hands are lifted high;*
> *my evening is dedicated to you.*
>
> My cry to you is urgent.
>
> So I beg you,
>   do not delay in answering my call.
> My prayer is rising before you now
>   like the burning of incense;
>   my hands are lifted high,
>   as a most serious evening oblation.
>
> Place a guard over my mouth,
>   like a sentry at the door of my lips.
> May evil words never sound forth from me;
>   may I never consider or choose
>   anything hateful or cruel.
> May I keep my distance
>   from the wicked
>   and never linger at their table.
>
> If someone just corrects me,
>   may I be humble enough
>   to receive it as a gracious kindness.

But may I never
    receive an anointing
    from evil sources;
    I pray that I will resist.

God, I turn myself totally toward you,
    for I only seek you for safety.
Keep me alive.
Do not let them trick me with traps
    they may set before me.
Let my foes receive their own fate.
But please,
    help me to escape their lost destiny.

(DH, adapt.)

Pause for Silent Prayer

Psalm 142

Safety—you are my safety.
You are all I have in this land of the living.

I am praying,
O dear God,
    I am praying.
    I am being hunted down
    and feel deserted by everyone.

I am surrendering my troubles;
    here they are,
    dripping down before you.

My breath
　　is getting shorter and shorter,
　　more faint
　　as I keep walking on this road
　　filled with traps
　　that are hidden everywhere.
Can you not see what is happening here?
No one seems to be my friend right now.

I have nowhere else to turn,
　　for I see no escape.
So I am turning to you,
　　my only route and path
　　to a land that is living.

Can you not hear me?
I am going hoarse
　　as I cry out to you.
Listen to me!
Rescue me!
I feel my foes closing in,
　　and I am frozen by my fear.

Set me free from this box!
For my freedom,
　　I will sing endlessly,
　　for I will most certainly know
　　that you are the one
　　who gave me back my life.

(DH, adapt.)

From Henri

Spirituality is attention
to the life of the spirit in us;

it is going out to the desert or up to the mountain
to pray;
it is standing before the Lord
with open heart and open mind;
it is crying out, "Abba, Father";
is contemplating the unspeakable beauty
of our loving God.

(HN, *The Living Reminder: Service and Prayer in
Memory of Jesus Christ*)

Silent Reflection

The Canticle of Mary

My soul is bursting with how great God is!
My spirit cannot stop rejoicing...

Prayers of Intercession

The Lord's Prayer

Sharing of the Peace / The Sign of the Cross

May God bless us, free us from all harm,
and lead us to life everlasting. Amen.

Sunday Morning Prayer

Invitatory / The Sign of the Cross

Optional Song or Hymn

Psalm 63:2–9

> *As this morning breaks through,*
> *I am looking to you to strengthen me.*

O God,
>> my ache is deep for you;
>> my soul and my body
>> are stretched to and beyond
>> my limit:
>> so dry,
>> so thirsty,
>> so desperate for you.

I am fixed on you
>> intensely,
>> right there—
>> in your holy place.

Radiant in strength.
Centered,
>> grounded in your glory.

The beauty of this life
>> cannot even claim a closeness
>> to the lavish presence
>> of your love.

I never can complete
    what is more
    than an entire lifetime of praise,
    with my arms and hands
    reaching out to you.
I am able to feast at this table,
    so rich in its flavor,
    feeding the song on my lips:
    glory!

All night long,
    I am awake,
    tossing and consumed
    with the memory of you—
    it fills my night.

You always help me,
    and I am here
    beneath your wings,
    lost in my rejoicing;
    I am clinging to you,
    knowing that your right hand
    will sustain me
    while the ground churns
    and turns
    beneath me.

Keeping me safe.

(DH, adapt.)

Pause for Silent Prayer

Psalm 149

*All of you who are God's faithful,
today is a day for a new song. Alleluia!*

Sing!
Come on, sing!
Not just any song,
>   but a NEW song—
>   a YOUNG song.

If you are among God's faithful,
>   then sing!

But be sure, however,
>   not to sing alone;
>   sing with each other,
>   with everyone gathered!

Find more, if possible;
>   find as many as you can
>   to join you in your song!

If they do not know how—
>   then teach them.

Israel—sing!
Zion—sing!

And along with your singing—
>   dance!
Dance in the name of God,
>   with instruments of all kinds
>   driving the rhythm!
Why?

Because our God
>   delights and revels in us—
>   all of us,
>   broken and in need of saving.

Every community,
>   every family:
>   join in.
As loudly as you can—
>   then nothing can defeat you!

Nothing.

Come on, you faithful ones:
>   sing!
This is your promise,
>   your glory!
There is no better response!

Alleluia!

(DH, adapt.)

From Henri

>   "Who am I as a living memory of God?"
>   The main question indeed
>   is not a question of doing,
>   but a question of being...
>   we need a spirituality,
>   a way of living in the spirit
>   by which all we are and all we do
>   becomes a form of reminding.

(HN, *The Living Reminder: Service and Prayer in Memory of Jesus Christ*)

Silent Reflection

The Canticle of Zachary

> God be blessed!
> I now am free, because I belong to God...

Prayers of Gratitude

The Lord's Prayer

Sharing of the Peace / The Sign of the Cross

> May God bless us, free us from all harm,
> and lead us to life everlasting. Amen.

Sunday Evening Prayer II

Invitatory / The Sign of the Cross

Optional Hymn or Song

Psalm 110:1, 3–4

> *You are to be raised over Zion and beyond.*
> *Alleluia!*

For all of us who dare to lead,
  we need to remember
  that any power that we have
  is grounded in God's covenant.

Only then
  will we have the loyalty of the people.

If we remember this,
  then the people will be one with us
  and stand with us.
Then our power is truly holy,
  renewed and fresh,
  and born again like the dawn.

God gives us this most blessed oath:

"You are my servant, forever;
  because I have made it so."

(DH, adapt.)

Pause for Silent Prayer

Psalm 114:7–8

All of you on earth, tremble before God.

Listen,
   all creatures of this earth:
Quiver!
Tremble!
Fear and honor God!

For here—
   here is your promised land!
Here is your ocean of mercy,
   flowing from what was once
   a stubborn, hard rock!

Now,
   all of our angry heat has melted!
This is the moment
   when our flint-edged hearts are transformed—
   bubbling up like young rivers!

(DH, adapt.)

From Henri

The minister is not called
to cheer people up
but modestly to remind them
that in the midst of pains and tribulations
the first sign of the new life can be found
and a joy can be experienced
which is hidden
in the midst of sadness.

(HN, *The Living Reminder: Service and Prayer in Memory of Jesus Christ*)

Silent Reflection

The Canticle of Mary

> My soul is bursting with how great God is!
> My spirit cannot stop rejoicing...

Prayers of Intercession

The Lord's Prayer

Sharing of the Peace / The Sign of the Cross

> May God bless us, free us from all harm,
> and lead us to life everlasting. Amen.

Monday Morning Prayer

Invitatory / The Sign of the Cross

Optional Song or Hymn

Psalm 5:2–4

> With the rising sun,
> I am praying to you, O God.
>
> Listen.
> Hear me.
> Bend your ear
>   and be the God you say you are;
>   Listen to my pierced heart!
>
> I keep praying,
>   as constant and sure
>   as the daybreak,
>   as the sun rises each day.
>
> At dawn
>   I continually place my prayer
>   before you.
>
> I am waiting.
>
> (DH, adapt.)

Pause for Silent Prayer

Psalm 29:1–4, 7–11

> *Honor the name of God.*
> *Give glory!*

Glory!
Give spirit-filled glory!
Glory beyond strength!
Honoring God!
Justice and holiness exploding!

Your voice
    is the voice of thundering,
    foaming waters!
Words that swell,
    voices that boom,
    all singing with glory!

Your ardent voice of fire:
    blasting forth with burning columns,
    shaking the wilderness,
    quaking the earth,
    scorching the trees,
    trembling with flames!

All speak of nothing but your power!

You speak above the mighty waters,
    creating a new flood
    of constancy and sovereignty!

You give strength to your people.
You bring peace to your people.
Blessing...

(DH, adapt.)

From Henri

Joy is essentially ecstatic
since it moves out of the place of death,
which is rigid and fixed,
and into the place of life
which is new and surprising....
There is no tinge of death in God.
God is pure life.

(HN, *Lifesigns: Intimacy, Fecundity, and
Ecstasy in Christian Perspective*)

Silent Reflection

The Canticle of Zachary

God be blessed!
I now am free, because I belong to God...

Prayers of Gratitude

The Lord's Prayer

Sharing of the Peace / The Sign of the Cross

May God bless us, free us from all harm,
and lead us to life everlasting. Amen.

Monday Evening Prayer

Invitatory / The Sign of the Cross

Optional Song or Hymn

Psalm 11:4–7

> *The poor know the tenderness of God.*

> God reclines in a temple of holiness,
>> and the heavens are steady in delight.
> God's eyes remain focused on us,
>> on all of us—
>> with no distinctions.
> God's gaze
>> keeps watch on the just and the wicked—
>> disowning and discrediting violence.
> God's response?
>> A storm of burning fire
>> with burning coals hurled at evil.

> Bottom line— God loves justice,
>> justice that restores.
> Then, and only then,
>> will we see the face of God.

(DH, adapt.)

Pause for Silent Prayer

Psalm 15

> *The pure of heart truly see God.*
> *They are blessed.*

God,
>who will you choose
>to welcome in close to you?
Who will you invite
>to live and dwell with you
>high above
>on your mountain of holiness?

Who?
The honest ones,
>the just ones,
>those who choose
>to reveal their hearts;
>those who refuse to lie,
>but insist on singing
>a song of truth.

Who?
The ones who cherish
>their sisters and brothers
>and who refuse
>to damage and slander them;
>those who honor
>their neighbor
>and who honor their God.

Who?
Those who keep promises
>no matter the cost;
>those who do not take advantage
>of the poor ones;
>those who accept no bribe
>to poison or harm another.

These—

> these are the ones
> who will never be swallowed up,
> who will never be shaken.

(DH, adapt.)

From Henri

> Prayer is such a radical act
> because it requires us
> to criticize our whole way of being in the world,
> to lay down our old selves,
> and to accept our new self,
> which is Christ.

(HN, *The Return of the Prodigal Son*)

Silent Reflection

The Canticle of Mary

> My soul is bursting with how great God is!
> My spirit cannot stop rejoicing...

Prayers of Intercession

The Lord's Prayer

Sharing of the Peace / The Sign of the Cross

> May God bless us, free us from all harm,
> and lead us to life everlasting. Amen.

Tuesday Morning Prayer

Invitatory / The Sign of the Cross

Optional Song or Hymn

Psalm 24:3–10

> *Those who have integrity*
> *shall be welcomed on God's mountain.*

Who is there among any of us
    who is worthy to crawl up
    to the mountain of God,
    stand at its top,
    and pray there—
    in the holiest of places?

The one whose hands are open,
    the one with a quiet heart,
    the one whose soul is freed up from lies,
    with no deceit to be found.

These are the ones
    who will be wrapped in blessing.
They are the ones
    who will receive
    the precious gift of God's justice.
These are the ones
    who constantly seek out
    God's presence,
    who are pulled into God's family
    and legacy.

Open up, gates of God!
Open up,
    stand strong
    and pave the way
    for the living,
    burning fire!

What is this fire?
Who is the source
    of this glorious heat?
    It is God,
    the all-powerful,
    and ever-final,
    lasting answer to chaos!

Open up, gates of God!
Open up!

What is this fire?
Who is the source
    of this glorious heat?
It is God,
    ever burning bright!

(DH, adapt.)

Pause for Silent Prayer

Psalm 33:4–9, 14–15, 18–19

*All who love justice,
sing and shout out your joy to God.*

God's word is true;
    God's words are what God does.
God loves justice and truth
    and fills the earth with deep love.

God speaks,
    and the heavens are created;
God breathes,
    and the stars brightly shine.
God bottles up the sea waters
    and keeps them in the deep.

Be astounded, O earth,
    and stand in honor of God.
God is speaking,
    and the world keeps on;
God is commanding,
    and all things are seen.

God looks down from heaven
    and takes notice of all people on the earth.
The creator of every human heart
    knows well every human action.

God's eye remains a loving constant
    on all who follow,
    on all those who look to God
    to bring safety in the midst of fear,
    to bring rescue in the midst of death.

With all we are and have,
    we wait for God,
    our helper and protection.
Our hearts are steeped in joy;
    we trust the name of God.

Come and love us, O God!
We are waiting.

(DH, adapt.)

From Henri

When I reflect on my own life,
I realize that the moments
of greatest comfort and consolation
were moments when someone said,
"I cannot take your pain away,
I cannot offer you a solution for your problem,
but I can promise you that I won't leave you alone
and will hold on to you
as long and as well as I can."

(HN, *Here and Now: Living in the Spirit*)

Silent Reflection

The Canticle of Zachary

God be blessed!
I now am free, because I belong to God …

Prayers of Gratitude

The Lord's Prayer

Sharing of the Peace / The Sign of the Cross

May God bless us, free us from all harm,
and lead us to life everlasting. Amen.

Tuesday Evening Prayer

Invitatory / The Sign of the Cross

Optional Song or Hymn

Psalm 20:8–9

> *Christ is God's victory for us.*

> Some people
>> brag and boast
>> about their weaponry
>> and their readiness
>> for battle.

> It is not so with us.

> We trust and we boast
>> in the name of God.
>> Nothing more.

> They will fall.
> We will rise up.

> (DH, adapt.)

Pause for Silent Prayer

Psalm 21:2–4a, 6

> *We sing, praise,*
> *and rejoice in your victory, O God.*

God,
> those who rule,
> those who lead,
> rejoice beyond rejoicing
> because of you,
> their strength.

> You infuse in them
>> the deep desire
>> of their hearts.

> You gift them with blessings.

> Your victories—
>> you do not keep them
>> to yourself.

> You hand them over,
>> to them,
>> to us.

(DH, adapt.)

From Henri

> Every moment of each day
> I have the chance to choose
> between cynicism and joy....
> Every word I speak can be cynical or joyful.
> Every action can be cynical or joyful.
> Increasingly I am aware of all these possible choices,

and increasingly I discover
that every choice for joy in turn
reveals more joy and offers more reason
to make life a true celebration...

(HN, *The Return of the Prodigal Son*)

Silent Reflection

The Canticle of Mary

My soul is bursting with how great God is!
My spirit cannot stop rejoicing...

Prayers of Intercession

The Lord's Prayer

Sharing of the Peace / The Sign of the Cross

May God bless us, free us from all harm,
and lead us to life everlasting. Amen.

Wednesday Morning Prayer

Invitatory / The Sign of the Cross

Optional Song or Hymn

Psalm 36:2–10

> *You are the fountain of life;*
> *come be our light, and we will see.*

> Evil conspires with evil.
> Sin gossips with those
> who choose darkness.
> Eyes are closed to God.
> Hearts are hardened
> and so cannot know.
> They cannot reject the dark.

> Words, then,
> mean nothing.
> They fall out the mouth—
> false and empty.
> They ignore goodness,
> revel in the crooked path,
> and hunt out
> things that sicken the soul.

> But your kindness, O God,
> reaches far into the darkness
> of every heart.
> Your integrity wins out,
> stretching tall and wide

over the mountain,
and your actions stir
like the waves of the sea.

You,
you delight in life!
You are the healing stream
that renews.
You are the light
that is opening our eyes again,
as if for the very first time!

We need your protection.
We are reaching out,
with the entirety of our hearts
to rest in the soothing warmth of your wings.
We come to be fed at your table.
We come,
choking on our tongues,
hoping to taste the cool refreshment
of your living stream.

You are our fountain of life.
In you— we see the light.

(DH, adapt.)

Pause for Silent Prayer

Psalm 47

Sing praise to God,
Sing to the one who reigns.

Bring your applause!
Clap your hands!
Give your affirmations

and acclamations of joy
to this incredible God of ours!

This God
    conquers and levels everything
    and everyone,
    gifting us with our land
    of dignity!

Our God,
    with ease,
    ascends to the top of the mountain
    accompanied
    by our blasts of the horn;
    by our cheers of thanksgiving;
    by our praise unending!

Sing praise, everyone—
    to our guide and direction,
    who does just that:
    this God is our compass.

So,
    sing out strong,
    to the ending point of your abilities!
Praise with everything
    you have
    and hope to be!

This God
    sits high
    but looks low,
    serving the people—
    God's holy people
    from every corner—

with every power unleashed
toward the glory of God!

(DH, adapt.)

From Henri

When we keep claiming the light,
we will find ourselves becoming
more and more radiant....
Every time we decide to be grateful
it will be easier to see new things
to be grateful for.

(HN, *Life of the Beloved*)

Silent Reflection

The Canticle of Zachary

God be blessed!
I now am free, because I belong to God...

Prayers of Gratitude

The Lord's Prayer

Sharing of the Peace / The Sign of the Cross

May God bless us, free us from all harm,
and lead us to life everlasting. Amen.

Wednesday Evening Prayer

Invitatory / The Sign of the Cross

Optional Song or Hymn

Psalm 27:1–6

> *God is our saving light;*
> *there is no need to be afraid.*

God is my living wall of light and safety.
I fear no one.
God is my sturdy protection,
    guiding my life—
    of whom could I ever be afraid?

When sources of darkness come together
    to frighten me,
    they fail;
    they stumble and fall.

My heart is not afraid
    of the forces that come after me;
    when all seems lost—
    even then,
    I trust.

Even then...

There is only one thing that I ask of God—
    one thing that I pray for:

to live out my life
in the house of God;
to every day
be taken up into the beauty of God,
to be pulled into prayer—
to be fused
and knitted tightly
within the fabric of God.

That would be more than enough.

God is relentless in keeping me safe—
from everything that desires harm,
from everyone who attempts to shatter
the rock that I am placed upon.

My head is raised high
above all people and things
that are trying to choke me.

I will offer God
my entire self,
joyfully,
making music,
singing endlessly.

(DH, adapt.)

Pause for Silent Prayer

Psalm 27:7–14

Do not hide from me, O God.
Show me your face.

God, hear me.

Be merciful.
Answer.
My heart is thirsting to see you.

I do not seek anyone, or anything,
    but for the gift and grace
    to see your blessed face.
Do not dismiss me—
you have always been my help.

Do not leave me alone!
Even if my mother and father abandon me—
    you will not.

It is impossible for you to forsake me.

Lead me, teach me your way.
Do not leave me alone with the toxic presence
    of my foes.

I believe, with everything I know,
    that your goodness will await me
    in the places that are alive!

Wait for God!
Be strong!

Wait for God!
(DH, adapt.)

From Henri

I have tried so hard in the past
to heal myself from my complaints and failed...
and failed...

and failed,
until I came to edge of complete emotional collapse
and even physical exhaustion.
I can only be healed from above,
from where God reaches down.
What is impossible for me is possible for God.

(HN, *The Return of the Prodigal Son*)

Silent Reflection

The Canticle of Mary

My soul is bursting with how great God is!
My spirit cannot stop rejoicing ...

Prayers of Intercession

The Lord's Prayer

Sharing of the Peace / The Sign of the Cross

May God bless us, free us from all harm,
and lead us to life everlasting. Amen.

Thursday Morning Prayer

Invitatory / The Sign of the Cross

Optional Song or Hymn

Psalm 57

> *Wake up the dawn!*
> *Awaken the music for God!*

> Bring your care, O God—
> take tender care with me
> as there is no place at all to hide.
> Surround me with the wings of your protection.

> You—you, God,
> are my avenger from heaven.
> Free me,
> and respond in kind to those who haunt me.

> Splash your tenderness upon me,
>   your love that never fails,
>   never relents.
> I am trapped with creatures
>   who crave to devour my body—
>   with cutting teeth,
>   with tongues like swords.

> Rise up above the sky!
> Spread your glory to across the earth.

They had strategies to bring me down—
    nets set,
    pits they had dug—
but they are the ones who have fallen in.

My heart is ready.
Decided.
Firm.
To you, I will sing my praise.

So everyone—
wake up the dawn!
Awaken the music for God!

My voice will come out of hiding
    and sing and praise
    only of you, and only for you.
Your love soars above and beyond my reach.

Rise up above the sky!
Spread your glory across the earth.

(DH, adapt.)

Pause for Silent Prayer

Psalm 48:9–15

Here in your house
we remember your love, O God.

What we can see,
    right here,
    lines up
    with all that we have been told:
    This is God's city,
    and God offers it protection,
    and lasting security.

God,
>we, the people of your city,
>call to mind
>and remember
>your tremendous,
>lasting love.

Our praise,
>like the holiness of your name,
>lasts forever
>and reaches
>to every known corner of the earth.

Your right hand
>holds the wonder of your justice.
Every mountain and city
>rejoices with abandon!

Move throughout Zion—
>move up and down,
>everywhere!
Take note of every tower
>and ponder deeply
>the mystery of these walls—
>consider and be curious about every inch
>of everything!

Then,
>you will be able to sing this song
>to your children:
>"God is here!
>God is everlasting!
>God cannot be stopped!
>God leads us
>against every kind of death—
>forever!"

(DH, adapt.)

From Henri

> Our lives are destined
> to become like the life of Jesus....
> Not only did Jesus come to free us
> from the bonds of sin and death,
> he also came to lead us into the intimacy
> of his divine life.

> (HN, *Making All Things New: An Invitation to the Spiritual Life*)

Silent Reflection

The Canticle of Zachary

> God be blessed!
> I now am free, because I belong to God...

Prayers of Gratitude

The Lord's Prayer

Sharing of the Peace / The Sign of the Cross

> May God bless us, free us from all harm,
> and lead us to life everlasting. Amen.

Thursday Evening Prayer

Invitatory / The Sign of the Cross

Optional Song or Hymn

Psalm 30:2–6, 11–13

> *I cried out to you, God. You healed me.*
> *I am relentless in my thanks.*

I want everyone to know
    and hear the praise
    that I wish to heap upon you,
    for you have brought color back to my life,
    after a time when there was nothing but grey.

The dim and dark will fail in their efforts.

When I was near the end of my breath,
    you came with healing.
You pulled and yanked me out of the quicksand,
    bringing me to safety.

My soul now rests.

I also want everyone to sing to your name,
    to your presence—bursting with thanks!
You will not hold on to anger,
    for you spread upon me the favor of your love.

Sleep may bring tears,
    but with my morning,
    I will be waking with you—
    joy-filled!

Take away the tears;
>   replace them with dancing and song.
>   Remove all that poisons,
>   and bring your balm of "happiness forever."

I cannot and will not remain silent.
My singing will continue;
>   my praise will be constant.
>   Your colors will brighten.

(DH, adapt.)

Pause for Silent Prayer

Psalm 32:7

> *God has pardoned us.*
> *Our happiness knows no bounds.*

You are my secret hiding place:
>   safety from suffering;
>   a freedom song;
>   an acclamation of rescue,
>   affirming my liberation.

(DH, adapt.)

From Henri

Everything that belongs to Jesus
is given for us to receive.
All that Jesus does we may also do.
Jesus does not speak about us
as second-class citizens.
He does not withhold anything from us....
Jesus wants us to be where he is.

(HN, *Making All Things New: An Invitation to the Spiritual Life*)

Silent Reflection

The Canticle of Mary

> My soul is bursting with how great God is!
> My spirit cannot stop rejoicing...

Prayers of Intercession

The Lord's Prayer

Sharing of the Peace / The Sign of the Cross

> May God bless us, free us from all harm,
> and lead us to life everlasting. Amen.

Friday Morning Prayer

Invitatory / The Sign of the Cross

Optional Song or Hymn

Psalm 51:12–19

All of Zion is made beautiful by your love.

Make clean and clear away
    all of the dust and debris
    from my heart.
Come and bring a steadiness,
    a smooth path to my spirit.
Do not abandon me—
    hold me tightly to your presence.

Help me,
    convince me
    that joy will follow pain.

Sustain and support me;
    and know
    that I will provide the direction
    to those who need
    to return to you.

Stop the tears
    so I will be able to sing a song
    love-packed with the taste of you.

Provide for my voice
    to clearly become a shout
    of praise to you.

Courage.
Bring courage to my heart.

Sacrifices will not work.
They do not satisfy you.
So then,
    I offer you my broken self:
    my fragile heart,
    my tender spirit.

These things you welcome.

You will not turn away,
    because you have my heart.

(DH, adapt.)

Pause for Silent Prayer

Psalm 100

Enter the door
with everlasting thanksgiving to God!

Break through!
Shout out, all the earth!

Serve!

With glad hearts—
    approach God and sing!

It is God—yes!
It is God who made us.

We belong to God;
    we are the flock who follows!

Come enter through the door
    with everlasting thanksgiving.

Come in, everyone,
    with singing to the name of God;
    Holy! Give thanks!

God's goodness never ends,
    and is faithful always.
From the beginning of life
    through the life after life,
    no one can put a stop
    to God's goodness,
    God's mercy,
    God's amazing love!

(DH, adapt.)

From Henri

Compassion means to become one
close to the one who suffers.
But we can come close to another person
only when we are willing to become vulnerable
ourselves.
A compassionate person says:
"I am your brother; I am your sister;
I am human, fragile, and mortal, just like you.
I am not scandalized by your tears,
nor afraid of your pain.
I too have wept. I too have felt pain."
We can be with the other
only when the other ceases to be "other"
and becomes like us.

(HN, *Here and Now: Living in the Spirit*)

46

Silent Reflection

The Canticle of Zachary

>God be blessed!
>I now am free, because I belong to God...

Prayers of Gratitude

The Lord's Prayer

Sharing of the Peace / The Sign of the Cross

>May God bless us, free us from all harm,
>and lead us to life everlasting. Amen.

Friday Evening Prayer

Invitatory / The Sign of the Cross

Optional Song or Hymn

Psalm 41:2–4, 14

> *God, I have failed you..*
> *Forgive me. Heal me.*

> Blessed are we
>> when we cannot wait
>> and are anxious
>> to reach out to the poor.
> God will then
>> shower us with generosity.

> God will not stop
>> shielding and protecting us
>> where we live—
>> our enemies
>> will not be able to get through
>> to bring us down.

> God will show us compassion
>> when we are ill—
>> we will be strengthened
>> in health
>> and in faith.

> Let us all, together:
>> bless this wonderful God!

Always.
Amen.

(DH, adapt.)

Pause for Silent Prayer

Psalm 46:9–12

*God's power is beyond all
and protects all.*

Pay attention!
See the wonder of God!
This God of ours
is everywhere,
destroying and crushing
all of the hatred and weaponry of war.

Stop the fighting—now!
God is coming to break the bows;
to silence the bullets and missiles;
to burn and destroy
the vehicles and wagons of violence.

Be still!
Enough.

(DH, adapt.)

From Henri

> Christian resistance is nonviolent,
> because the peace we want to bring
> is not of this world.
> It is brought not by enslaving our enemies,
> but by converting them;
> not by showing strength,
> but by sharing in the confession of a common
> weakness;
> not by becoming unapproachable,
> but by making oneself vulnerable;
> not by retaliation,
> but by turning the other cheek;
> not by violence,
> but by love.

(HN, *Peacework: Prayer, Resistance, Community*)

Silent Reflection

The Canticle of Mary

> My soul is bursting with how great God is!
> My spirit cannot stop rejoicing...

Prayers of Intercession

The Lord's Prayer

Sharing of the Peace / The Sign of the Cross

> May God bless us, free us from all harm,
> and lead us to life everlasting. Amen.

Saturday Morning Prayer

Invitatory / The Sign of the Cross

Optional Song or Hymn

Psalm 119:145–152

> *In the chill of the night I ache for your presence.*

With a heart so full,
    I ache for you to hear me.
Bring the freedom I seek
    so I may follow you.

I have turned my face to you
    during the cold of the night,
    waiting,
    praying,
    to hear from you.

Throughout the night I have kept vigil,
    lingering,
    pondering,
    musing upon your promises.

Listen to me,
    you, the "God who loves";
    may I live by your justice.
Those who want to cause harm
    are closing in.

But you, God,
    you even closer, so very close.
Your way shines with truth!

Since I was young
I have learned these things about you,
and they are rooted in me forever.

(DH, adapt.)

Pause for Silent Prayer

Psalm 117

Praise! Glory!
Every people of every nation—sing glory!

Praise!
From every land,
from every throat,
from the deepest heart,
from all people—
praise!

And yes, glory!
Glory to God!

The love is so strong,
so embracing,
so faithful.

Without end.
Infinite.

Now, praise that!

(DH, adapt.)

From Henri

It is indeed a hard discipline
to be useless in God's presence
and to let him speak in the silence of my heart.

But whenever I become a little useless
I know God is calling me to a new life
far beyond the boundaries of my usefulness.

(HN, *The Living Reminder: Service and Prayer in
Memory of Jesus Christ*)

Silent Reflection

The Canticle of Zachary

God be blessed!
I now am free, because I belong to God…

Prayers of Gratitude

The Lord's Prayer

Sharing of the Peace / The Sign of the Cross

May God bless us, free us from all harm,
and lead us to life everlasting. Amen.

WEEK TWO

The real "work" of prayer
is to become silent
and listen to the voice
that says good things about me.

(HN, *Life of the Beloved*)

Sunday Evening Prayer I

Invitatory / The Sign of the Cross

Optional Song or Hymn

Psalm 119:105–122

> *Your word enlightens my path.*

Your word is a blazing torch
    to create a path—
    a light for me to follow.
My loyalty is to you.

I have suffered;
    come and restore my life.
You promised.
Hear what I am crying out to you,
    and teach me.

Though danger comes at me from every side,
    your path is never far from my heart.
Those who choose to harm me
    will not deter my focus on you.
I will not stray.

Your way is my choice and destiny,
    and my heart rejoices.
I am committed and determined;
I will keep saying "yes."
You are my prize.

(DH, adapt.)

Pause for Silent Prayer

56

Psalm 16:1–2a, 5–8, 11

You reveal to me the direction for my life.
My joy is boundless.

Glorious God, protect me.
I turn to you alone for help.
You are my God,
    my all, and my greatest good.

God, you are my portion and cup,
    and you give shape to my future.
You set aside for me the best of places,
    to celebrate my heritage.

I offer blessing to my God
    who, even at night,
      teaches me, strengthens me.
God is here;
I am sure of it.
Right here, by my side.

My heart is ongoing,
    always lifted, always rejoicing.
My body is quaking,
    thrilled with breath—
      at rest.

Safe.

God, you reveal to me
    the only direction that I need—
    the path to life.

Joy to the most wonderful and extreme,
    at your side.
    Now and always.

(DH, adapt.)

From Henri

Since my vocation, like Peter's,
is to be led where Jesus wants me to
"feed [his] sheep,"
I have to be willing to lay down my life for them.
This might in special circumstances
mean dying for others,
but it means first of all making our own lives—
our sorrows and joys, our despair and hope,
our loneliness and experience of intimacy—
available to others as sources of new life.
One of the greatest gifts we can give to others is
ourselves.

(HN, *Discernment: Reading the Signs of Daily Life*)

Silent Reflection

The Canticle of Mary

My soul is bursting with how great God is!
My spirit cannot stop rejoicing...

Prayers of Intercession

The Lord's Prayer

Sharing of the Peace / The Sign of the Cross

May God bless us, free us from all harm,
and lead us to life everlasting. Amen.

Sunday Morning Prayer

Invitatory / The Sign of the Cross

Optional Song or Hymn

Psalm 118:1–4, 10–14

> *Blessed is the one who comes in God's name.*

Praise and unending thanksgiving
    be to you:
        For your mercy pierces through!

Let all who struggle and suffer,
    speak and celebrate:
        For your mercy pierces through!

Let the house of Aaron,
    and every house,
    speak and celebrate:
        For your mercy pierces through!

Let all who honor your name,
    speak and celebrate:
        For your mercy pierces through!

The nations from every corner
    engulf and attempt to swallow me:
        But by your name, I cut them off!

They surround me like bees
    threatening to sting:
        But by your name, I cut them off!

They plot to blaze up
>a thorn-filled fire:
>>But by your name, I cut them off!

They thrust into me
>deeply and with the intent of death.
But you,
>you protect me.

You are my song
>that keeps me strong.
You are my song
>of compassion and rescue.

(DH, adapt.)

Pause for Silent Prayer

Psalm 150

God's deeds demand praise!
Praise God!

You!

Praise You!
You in your home!
You in the heavens!

You!

Strong!
Holy!
Deeds upon deeds!

You!

Power from the trumpets!
Glory from the many strings!

Harps with glissandos!
Justice dancing!
Drums pounding!
Timbrels clanging!
Pipes blasting!

You!

Joy from crashing cymbals!
Ecstasy from ringing!
Endless bell overtones!
Everything resonating!
Everything breathing fully and clearly!
Everything alive!

You!

(DH, adapt.)

From Henri

You, like Christ, are God's beloved child.
In you, God is well pleased.
Your belovedness precedes your birth.
It will follow you all the days of your life and
beyond death.
You are fully loved of God before your father and
mother,
brother, sister, family, or church loved you or didn't
love you,
hurt you or helped you.
You are fully loved because you belong to God for
all eternity.
That the truth of your identity.
That's who you are.
And you can reclaim it at any moment.

(HN, *Spiritual Formation: Following the
Movements of the Spirit*)

Silent Reflection

The Canticle of Zachary

> God be blessed!
> I now am free, because I belong to God…

Prayers of Intercession

The Lord's Prayer

Sharing of the Peace / The Sign of the Cross

> May God bless us, free us from all harm,
> and lead us to life everlasting. Amen.

Sunday Evening Prayer II

Invitatory / The Sign of the Cross

Optional Song or Hymn

Psalm 110 1, 3–4

> *Christ is our sovereign. Always.*

For all of us who dare to lead,
we need to remember
that any power that we have
is grounded in God's covenant.

Only then
will we have the loyalty of the people.

If we remember this,
then the people will be one with us,
and stand with us.
Then our power is truly holy,
renewed and fresh,
and born again like the dawn.

God gives us this most blessed oath:

"You are my servant, forever;
because I have made it so."

(DH, adapt.)

Pause for Silent Prayer

Psalm 115

All who believe will receive God's blessing.
Everyone!

Open eyes!
> Open eyes for all to see,
> but not to us, no—
> not to us—
> but because of your love,
> impossible to name;
> because of your truth,
> incapable of flaws.

Why should anyone even say or think,
> "Where is your God?"

Our God is without fault or excuse,
> abiding, in hidden things,
> accomplishing all that is held desirable.

Our God need not answer to anyone.

For some,
> their idols or "gods"
> are made of hands,
> measly silver and gold,
> nothing special.

Because they come
> from mouths that are mute,
> eyes that cannot see,
> ears that cannot begin to hear,
> and noses completely unable
> to sense the scents.

They have hands
>that are unable to feel or touch,
>feet that cannot make the journey,
>throats that are completely silent,
>with nothing to say.

They utter nothing.

And their makers—
>nothing different at all;
>all the same.

You who struggle,
>trust the presence of the One
>you cannot see—
>who is our help and protection.
Let the house of Aaron and every other house,
>begin to trust.

You, God,
>are constantly mindful of us.

Bless us.
Bless those who struggle.
Bless the house of Aaron,
>all of Israel,
>and all of us who revere you.

All of us,
>great and small—
>may we be blessed,
>blessed by the hand of the One
>who fashions both heaven and earth!

God, you belong to all who live!
Here and now, on the earth!
Those who are dead cannot praise you,
    nor those who have gone silent.

But for us,
        for us—
        we sing!

Always!
With careless abandon!
Toward all of our tomorrows!

Alleluia!

(DH, adapt.)

From Henri

The pains and struggles
we encounter in our solitude
thus become the way to hope,
because our hope is not based on something
that will happen after our sufferings are over,
but on the real presence
of God's healing Spirit
in the midst of these sufferings.

(HN, *Making All Things New: An Invitation to the
Spiritual Life*)

Silent Reflection

The Canticle of Mary

My soul is bursting with how great God is!
My spirit cannot stop rejoicing...

Prayers of Intercession

The Lord's Prayer

Sharing of the Peace / The Sign of the Cross

> May God bless us, free us from all harm,
> and lead us to life everlasting. Amen.

Monday Morning Prayer

Invitatory / The Sign of the Cross

Optional Song or Hymn

Psalm 42:2–4, 6

> *I am thirsting and aching fog God.*
> *When will I see God's face?*
>
> Thirsting.
> Craving.
> Gasping.
> Just as a deer reaches for water,
>   I reach—
>   I ache for you.
> Will you come?
> When will I see you?
>
> Dry soul.
> Tears— my drink.
> My litany,
>   my crying out is endless:
>   where are you?
>
> Why is my soul so sad?
> Why the endless tears?
> I can still long for you.
> I can wait.
> I can still praise.

(DH, adapt.)

Pause for Silent Prayer

Psalm 19:2–7

The skies above sing of God's glory.

You have made such glory!

The heavens are the accomplishment
    of your creative touch.

From the beginning of one day
    to the other
    your voice is clear;
    from night to night,
    your insight is made known.

There are no words!
There is no way to verbalize,
    express, or sing adequately of such things.
They are but sounds
    that move about everywhere
to every corner of the earth;
    they are profound utterances of grace
    going forth to every edge.

You place a canopy for the sun—
    never missing the bride.
You run from beginning to finish
    as a champion would,
    faster, and yet so deliberately complete.

From the starting point—
    the sun is heating up, rising,
    and like the runner,

it reaches its goal, its course.
For there is nothing that can be hidden
    from these burning flames of glory!

God of all beginnings!
Only beginnings!

(DH, adapt.)

From Henri

Prayer means entering into communion
with the One who loved us before we could love.
It is this "first love"
that is revealed to us in prayer.
The more deeply we enter into the house of God,
the house whose language is prayer,
the less dependent we are
on the blame or praise of those who surround us,
and the freer we are
to let our whole being be filled with that first love.

(HN, *The Return of the Prodigal Son*)

Silent Reflection

The Canticle of Zachary

God be blessed!
I now am free, because I belong to God...

Prayers of Gratitude

The Lord's Prayer

Sharing of the Peace / The Sign of the Cross

May God bless us, free us from all harm,
and lead us to life everlasting. Amen.

Monday Evening Prayer

Invitatory / The Sign of the Cross

Optional Song or Hymn

Psalm 45:2–10

> No other beauty comes close; no other words are
> adequate:
> God has blessed us so lavishly!

My heart is so full—
    almost too full
    (though that seems impossible)
    of songs,
    of melodies and harmonies,
    of rhythms,
    of music
    to praise you.

Know this:
    I will not hold back;
    I will lift my voice
    with all my skill
    to announce you—
    my song of love.

You are my hero;
    you are the one
    who takes up the sword of protection.
Blaze the way
    and slay all things that deny your truth:
    pierce all that seeks to deny justice to the poor.
Do not shrink from displaying your power.

Your tools for this justice are ready—
    nations will shrink to your power;
    the foes of justice will lose their steam.

Your rule, your justice
    is as lasting as God is lasting.
Integrity.

You love justice.
You despise evil.
God has anointed you
with the oil of festival and gladness.

What you wear— is fragrant with God's beauty.
Music soars to welcome you
    to the palace of God's reign—
    and your heart is glad.

You are honored by the queen at your right hand.
You are arrayed in gold.

(DH, adapt.)

Pause for Silent Prayer

Psalm 30:2–6, 11:13

My soul now rests.

I want everyone to know
    and hear the praise
    that I wish to heap upon you,
    for you have brought color back to my life,
    after a time when there was nothing but grey.

The dim and dark will fail in their efforts.

When I was near the end of my breath,
     you came with healing.
You pulled and yanked me out of the quicksand
     bringing me to safety.

My soul now rests.

I also want everyone to sing to your name,
     to your presence—bursting with thanks!
You will not hold on to anger,
     for you spread upon me the favor of your love.

Sleep may bring tears,
     but with my morning,
     I will be waking with you—
     joy-filled!

Take away the tears;
     replace them with dancing and song.
     Remove all that poisons,
     and bring your balm of "happiness forever."

I cannot and will not remain silent.
My singing will continue,
     my praise will be constant.
     Your colors will brighten.

O God, keep me free...

(DH, adapt.)

From Henri

Compassion is not mine
but God's gift to me.
I cannot embrace the world,

but God can.
I cannot pray, but God can pray in me.
When God became as we are,
that is,
when God allowed all of us
to enter into his intimate life,
it became possible for us to share
in his infinite compassion.

(HN, *The Genesee Diary: Report from a Trappist Monastery*)

Silent Reflection

The Canticle of Mary

My soul is bursting with how great God is!
My spirit cannot stop rejoicing...

Prayers of Intercession

The Lord's Prayer

Sharing of the Peace / The Sign of the Cross

May God bless us, free us from all harm,
and lead us to life everlasting. Amen.

Tuesday Morning Prayer

Invitatory / The Sign of the Cross

Optional Song or Hymn

Psalm 43:1–2

> *Send light, send truth.*

God,
>> make your loving decisions for me,
>> on my behalf.
> Be my defense,
>> and present my case
>> to those who are cruel;
>> those who want to hurt me.

> For you are
>> my single,
>> my most faithful,
>> and my most trusted fortress.

(DH, adapt.)

Pause for Silent Prayer

Psalm 65:6–9

> *All of our praise is a joyous song to you, O God.*

> You have won the victory,
>> giving completion to our prayers.
> You alone
>> are awesome beyond

the hope of peace
on both land and water.

With your own strength
you have steadied the fragile mountains,
and stilled the noises of the sea.
The waves that argue with each other,
the nations that rage against each other,
all troubling things
are made quiet and calm.

Everyone, everywhere
is in awe of you and your work.
From one edge of the earth
to the other,
joy fills and explodes in all things—
its shouts cannot be silenced.

(DH, adapt.)

From Henri

To give someone a blessing
is the most significant affirmation we can offer.
It is more than a phrase of appreciation;
it is more than praising another's gifts or good
deeds.
To give a blessing
is to affirm another's core identity,
to say yes to a person's belovedness.

(HN, *Discernment: Reading the Signs of Daily Life*)

Silent Reflection

The Canticle of Zachary

> God be blessed!
> I now am free, because I belong to God...

Prayers of Gratitude

The Lord's Prayer

Sharing of the Peace / The Sign of the Cross

> May God bless us, free us from all harm,
> and lead us to life everlasting. Amen.

Tuesday Evening Prayer

Invitatory / The Sign of the Cross

Optional Song or Hymn

Psalm 49:2–5, 14–15, 16

> *Only God can liberate us.*

All of you,
     yes, you...
     sit up,
     pay attention,
     and listen to me.

All of you,
     the lowly, the rich,
     all who are needy—
     be attentive:

I have to share this wisdom with you,
     for I can see clearly
     and directly.
My ear leans toward what is true,
     and I want to sing it from the rooftop!

Those only concerned with themselves—
     they are lost,
     and will find themselves in darkness.

But this I know—
     yes, I really know:
     God is my rescue.
     God will guide my soul.

Even amidst the stench of death,
    I will be lifted up.
    I will remain fresh and free.

(DH, adapt.)

Pause for Silent Prayer

Psalm 120

God, be our peace.
Bring us to peace.

Right now—only distress.
Right now—only anguish.
Right now—only this most lonely hour.

So I call out to you.
You have answered.
You are present.

This is my cry,
    right now:
    "God, save and protect me
    from those who are scheming against me!"

So, to you,
    you who are scheming:
    How do you think God
    will reward you?
Keep sharp and look out
    for the even sharper arrows
    and hot coals that come your way!

Why do I have to wander
    and remain in such harmful places,
    with those who want only violence?

I am speaking for peace.
They seem to be continually
    speaking of war.

(DH, adapt.)

From Henri

I find it difficult to conceive
of a more concrete way to love
than by praying for one's enemies.
It makes you conscious of the hard fact
that in God's eyes,
you're no more and no less worthy of being loved
than any other person,
and it creates an awareness of profound solidarity
with all other human beings.

(HN, *Letters to Marc About Jesus: Living a
Spiritual Life in a Material World*)

Silent Reflection

The Canticle of Mary

My soul is bursting with how great God is!
My spirit cannot stop rejoicing...

Prayers of Intercession

The Lord's Prayer

Sharing of the Peace / The Sign of the Cross

May God bless us, free us from all harm,
and lead us to life everlasting. Amen.

Wednesday Morning Prayer

Invitatory / The Sign of the Cross

Optional Song or Hymn

Psalm 77:1–10

> *God, you alone are the holy one.*
> *There is no other god that can compare to you.*

My eyes,
    my heart—
    feel nothing but torment.
My soul is refusing
    any comfort or peace.

I think of you,
    and I cannot stop moaning.
During the day, I keep aching for you.
During the night, I keep reaching out,
    and I feel as though you are not grabbing on.

My spirit is crushed
    when I think of my life.
You seem to render me mute
    when I long to speak.

I remember the past,
    the times and days gone by—
    mistakes, wrong choices,
    repressed joy,
    acts of shame.

It all haunts me.

Are you prepared
    to leave me here alone,
    rejected forever?
Have you stopped loving me?

Have you forgotten
    to be merciful?

Is your anger that hot?

No hope for restoration?
No healing?

(DH, adapt.)

Pause for Silent Prayer

Psalm 97:1-6, 11–12

God alone rules;
joy reaches everywhere.

God reigns!
Everyone and everything on earth
    can taste it!

God is here!
The clouds gather to rain down,
    to drench the earth with integrity!

God is blazing!
Flickering and moving,
    burning up all that try to resist!

God sees!
The mountains and hills melt

and begin to slip away—
the flames clarify everything,
clearing the brush,
creating a path!

God is loud!
With justice and righteousness
exploding wide open,
reaching everywhere!

God blooms!
Light sprinkles about,
bringing joy to every heart
eager for what is right.

We can see it!
Give thanks!

(DH, adapt.)

From Henri

The question is not
"How am I to find God?"
but "How am I to let myself be found by him?"
The question is not
"How am I to know God"
but "How am I to let myself be known by God?"
And, finally,
the question is not
"How am I to love God?"
but "How am I to let myself be loved by God?"
God is looking into the distance for me,
trying to find me,
and longing to bring me home.

(HN, *The Return of the Prodigal Son*)

Silent Reflection

The Canticle of Zachary

> God be blessed!
> I now am free, because I belong to God...

Prayers of Gratitude

The Lord's Prayer

Sharing of the Peace / The Sign of the Cross

> May God bless us, free us from all harm,
> and lead us to life everlasting. Amen.

Wednesday Evening Prayer

Invitatory / The Sign of the Cross

Optional Song or Hymn

Psalm 62

> *Wait. Be still, and keep silent for God,*
> *our only hope.*
>
> My soul is resting only in God,
>> and in no one else.
> God alone saves and completes me;
>> my sturdy foundation, my safety,
>> my saving wall, my security.
>
> How much longer will one be attacked?
> How much more will one be beaten down,
>> as if a flimsy wall
>> or a weak and fragile fence?
>
> My soul is resting only in God,
>> in no one else.
> God is my solitary source of hope.
> God alone saves and completes me—
>> my sturdy foundation, my safety,
>> my saving wall, my security.
>
> Glory and safety—only in God.
> Strength and refuge—only in God.
> My friends, put your trust in this God,
>> always.

Let your hearts be poured out freely
at the feet of this God.

Why?

Because this God,
    this God,
    is the only true fountain of safety and rescue.

(DH, adapt.)

Pause for Silent Prayer

Psalm 67

Show us your favor and care, O God.
Shine your face upon us.

Care for us.
Bless us.
Shine your face upon us.
Reveal yourself to us.
Bear life in us.
Bring out praise in us.

Let all the earth know
    how you keep breathing in us;
    how you continually
    guide all creation;
    everyone, everything
    follows you
    to your destination,
    your land of justice,
    your resting place of honor.

The richness of the land
    sprouts forth the harvest—
O God,
    how you have blest us!

Do not relent—
    keep the blessings coming!
And may we all
    embrace and make known
    our prayer of praise—
    our worship to you.

(DH, adapt.)

From Henri

To the degree that our prayer
has become the prayer of our heart
we will love more and suffer more,
we will see more light and more darkness,
more grace and more sin,
more of God and more of humanity.
To the degree that we have descended into our heart
and reached out to God from there,
solitude can speak to solitude,
deep to deep and heart to heart.
It is there where love and pain are found together.

(HN, *Reaching Out: The Three Movements of the Spiritual Life*)

Silent Reflection

The Canticle of Mary

My soul is bursting with how great God is!
My spirit cannot stop rejoicing...

Prayers of Intercession

The Lord's Prayer

Sharing of the Peace / The Sign of the Cross

May God bless us, free us from all harm,
and lead us to life everlasting. Amen.

Thursday Morning Prayer

Invitatory / The Sign of the Cross

Optional Song or Hymn

Psalm 80:2–3, 25–26, 18–29

> *Be our strength, O God.*
> *Come and protect us— be our shepherd.*

Turn our hearts around.
Shine.
Enlighten.
Open us up.

Listen, and be our shepherd.
You live in the distance
    with the angels—
      come close!
Shine, and don't hold back,
    keep the light beaming!

Come back to us,
    come down from your heights
    and think of us—
    we, your vine—
    and water us,
    protect us,
    for you are the one who planted us.
Our roots are dug deep in you.

Reach down with your right hand

upon us,
your chosen,
who are strong,
all because of you.

We will not turn from you.
Breathe your life
back into our breath,
and we will call out to the world,
singing and celebrating you,
and you alone.

Come, now.
Revive.

(DH, adapt.)

Pause for Silent Prayer

Psalm 81:2–4

Keep shouting your joy!
God is our strength.

I keep singing.
I keep singing to you,
God,
my unending strength.

I chant my psalm to you,
and I do so
with all my heart.

I strike the drum,
    strum the strings,
    and I blow the horn
    at the New Moon!

For this is the appointed day,
    a time for feasting!

(DH, adapt.)

From Henri

Getting answers to my questions
is not the goal of the spiritual life.
Living in the presence of God
is the greater call.

(HN, *Discernment: Reading the Signs of Daily Life*)

Silent Reflection

The Canticle of Zachary

God be blessed!
I now am free, because I belong to God...

Prayers of Gratitude

The Lord's Prayer

Sharing of the Peace / The Sign of the Cross

May God bless us, free us from all harm,
and lead us to life everlasting. Amen.

Thursday Evening Prayer

Optional Song or Hymn

Psalm 72:1–4, 12–14

> *You are light to all the nations.*

God,
> come now
> and make your position clear:
> justice for the poor—
> nothing less!

May the mountain of your love
> bring peace to the people.

Come now,
> protect your cause,
> your poor ones;
> save the needy—
> bring a stop to the oppression!

We are holding you to your word—
> that you will deliver those
> who are crying out;
> that you will show your compassion
> to the desperate
> and the helpless.

Not someday,
> not some distant future possibility...

come now!
Come and save all the broken.
End the violence!

Redeem!

Rescue the ones
　　whom we know and believe
　　you love so dearly.

(DH, adapt.)

Pause for Silent Prayer

Psalm 73:1–3, 21–26

You, O God,
are the center of my heart.

I know and can trust God
　　when my heart is clear,
　　and has not grown complicated
　　and distracted;
　　when it can beat lovingly,
　　undeterred from the confusion
　　that can undo so much.

I come so close
　　to stumbling;
　　too often
　　I slip and almost crash to the ground.
My balance can be shaken,
　　when the arrogance of the proud
　　plays the trick,
　　triggers me,
　　and hooks me in.

And so,
    my heart turned hard.
My soul—cold.
My being allowed my anger
    to sour my spirit;
    and I felt the bite of envy.
I was so foolish.
I was blind,
    so unable to see—
    so stupid.

But I returned to you.
You have taken me
    by my right hand,
    and guided me into your house,
    and shared with me
    a daily awareness of you.
And here, I know the song:
    the song is "Glory!"

With you, here,
    delighting my life
    on this earth,
    what need have I of heaven?

Even if my body,
    heart, and mind fail me,
    I have you.

For you—
    you are my heart's center.

You are my everlasting strength.

(DH, adapt.)

From Henri

The great challenge is *living* your wounds through
instead of *thinking* them through.
It is better to cry than to worry,
better to feel your wounds deeply than to
understand them,
better to let them enter into your silence
than to talk about them.
The choice you face constantly
is whether you are taking to your hurts to your head
or to your heart…
You need to let your wounds go down into your heart.
Then you can live through them and discover
that they will not destroy you.
Your heart is greater than your wounds.

(HN, *The Inner Voice of Love: A Journey through
Anguish to Freedom*)

Silent Reflection

The Canticle of Mary

My soul is bursting with how great God is!
My spirit cannot stop rejoicing…

Prayers of Intercession

The Lord's Prayer

Sharing of the Peace / The Sign of the Cross

May God bless us, free us from all harm,
and lead us to life everlasting. Amen.

Friday Morning Prayer

Invitatory / The Sign of the Cross

Optional Song or Hymn

Psalm 51:12–19

> *O God, you celebrate our hearts made new.*

Make clean and clear away
    all of the dust and debris
    from my heart.
Come and bring a steadiness,
    a smooth path to my spirit.
Do not abandon me—
    hold me tightly to your presence.

Help me,
    convince me
    that joy will follow pain.

Sustain and support me;
    and know
    that I will provide the direction
    to those who need
    to return to you.

Stop the tears
    so I will be able to sing a song
    love-packed with the taste of you.

Provide for my voice
    to clearly become a shout
    of praise to you.

Courage.
Bring courage to my heart.

Sacrifices will not work.
They do not satisfy you.
So then,
>   I offer you my broken self:
>   my fragile heart,
>   my tender spirit.

These things you welcome.

You will not turn away,
>   because you have my heart.

(DH, adapt.)

Pause for Silent Prayer

Psalm 147:12–16, 19–20

>   *Jerusalem, give glory!*

Listen well, Jerusalem!
Zion, be attentive and praise!

God has kept you safe,
>   for you are locked in and protected;
>   provided with children,
>   peaceful in your homes,
>   and fed well with the finest of wheat.

God continues to speak:
>   Word proclaimed, spoken, shouted!
>   Snow sprinkles down like diamonds;
>   frost sows like the dust
>   and is scattered about
>   chased away by the melting wind.

God speaks the Word;
   to all of you, the direction is given.
You alone, O Jacob,
   are the landing point and target
   for God's voice.

No one else can hear!

(DH, adapt.)

From Henri

Gratitude...
goes beyond the "mine" and "thine"
and claims the truth that all of life is a pure gift.
In the past I always thought of gratitude
as a spontaneous response
to the awareness of gifts received,
but now I realize that gratitude
can also be lived as a discipline.
The discipline of gratitude
is the explicit effort to acknowledge
that all I am and have is given to me
as a gift of love,
a gift to be celebrated with joy.

(HN, *The Return of the Prodigal Son*)

Silent Reflection

The Canticle of Zachary

God be blessed!
I now am free, because I belong to God...

Prayers of Gratitude

The Lord's Prayer

Sharing of the Peace / The Sign of the Cross

> May God bless us, free us from all harm,
> and lead us to life everlasting. Amen.

Friday Evening Prayer

Invitatory / The Sign of the Cross

Optional Song or Hymn

Psalm 116:1–9

> *God is my rising from death.*
>
> I so love God...
>   for I have been heard.
> God leans toward me
>   to hear my voice when I call.
>
> Death nearly had me,
>   my grave was prepared,
>   and anguish took hold of me.
> I cried out to God,
>   "Rescue me!"
>
> God was and is, kind.
> God was and is, faithful.
> God was and is, gentle.
> God protects the poor
>   and pulls me out of the dust.
>
> Rest again, O my heart,
>   for God's love is here.
> God will not let me die;
>   my tears will end,
>   and my feet will be steady.
> I will know the presence of God
>   in this land that lives!

(DH, adapt.)

Pause for Silent Prayer

Psalm 121

God is my help,
the maker of the earth and the heavens.

The mountains hold my gaze;
    it is there where I find my help.
God provides my strength.
God opens wide heaven and earth.

God will keep you steady
    when you begin to stumble,
    never sleeping while keeping watch.
God refuses to sleep
    while holding guard over you, blessed Israel.

Protection and shade—
    God provides at your right hand.
The sun will not blind your day.
The moon will not harm your night.

God will always keep you safe from harm;
    your soul will be kept safe.
God will watch over your movements,
    your comings and goings.

Always.

(DH, adapt.)

From Henri

If you live with hope,
you can live very much in the present

because you can nurture the footprints of God
in your heart and life.
You already have a sense of what is to come.
And the whole of the spiritual life
is saying that God is right with us, right now.

("*A Tribute to Henri Nouwen.*")

Silent Reflection

The Canticle of Mary

My soul is bursting with how great God is!
My spirit cannot stop rejoicing...

Prayers of Intercession

The Lord's Prayer

Sharing of the Peace / The Sign of the Cross

May God bless us, free us from all harm,
and lead us to life everlasting. Amen.

Saturday Morning Prayer

Invitatory / The Sign of the Cross

Optional Song or Hymn

Psalm 92

> *How good it is to greet the morning*
> *in your love and presence.*

It is so good,
>> even though it is challenging—
>> to give thanks and praise
>> to your unsayable name.

In the morning light
>> we remember
>> your amazing kindness;
>> with the night sky
>> we call to mind and ponder
>> your most faithful heart.

We sing about these things,
>> and so much more,
>> with every instrument
>> we can get our hands on,
>> because every deed of yours
>> demands a song!

Every thing you do
>> is stunning;
>> you are at work in everything,

and we become animated
by your stirrings—
too deep to comprehend!

To not be taken in by you
is to be so utterly foolish.
There are scoundrels out there,
springing up like weeds.
They begin to bloom,
but they cannot sustain any growth—
thus they are mowed down.

But you cannot be mowed down
because those who oppose you
are scattered and cast away.

You strengthen us,
and anoint us with new resolve:
we glisten and grow;
brighten and glow;
and are given fresh eyes
so we can see clearly;
fresh ears
so we can hear
and tune out
the noise of those who bring harm.

So we will grow justly
like palm trees!
We will rise up majestically

like the cedars of Lebanon!
We will be planted in your house,
 our leaves eternally green,
 rustling in your courtyard.

Even though we will grow old,
 our branches will flourish,
 stay vigorous,
 covered with foliage.

We will remain your emblem of justice.
We will be sealed
 with no possible cracks to be found.

(DH, adapt.)

Pause for Silent Prayer

Psalm 8

Your name is so beautiful,
so wonderful and great.

It is impossible
 to pin you down,
 to contain you,
 to name you adequately.

Your name is too beautiful
 and filled with glory—
 it moves and dances
 beyond my sight,
 beyond my mind,
 landing and stirring in my heart.

Your presence—

extends beyond imagination
to imagination,
mystery bound,
always outward,
further and further
beyond my senses,
beyond the planets and stars.

Even the mouths of the newborn
make their wordless sounds to you:
strength too impossible to fathom,
power too mighty to ponder;
enemies brought down.

I behold the night sky
and the work of your hands:
the bright moon
and the sparkling stars
that you made.

And then I think:

Who is woman,
so frail—
that you remember her?
Who is man,
so small—
that you keep him in mind?
Who are any of us,
so insignificant—
that you care at all?

But beyond all reason,
you hold us all as angels,
as gods,
as holy!

You have crowned us
    in your own splendor.
You have empowered us
    to take charge,
    to take care of your creation:

Sheep and cattle,
    flocks of birds
    and herds of deer,
    the goats and the cows,
    and the fish
    who dart about in the sea.

Your name is too beautiful
    and filled with glory!

(DH, adapt.)

From Henri

If God forgives the sinners,
then certainly those who have faith in God should
do the same.
If God welcomes sinners home,
then certainly those who trust in God should do
likewise.
If God is compassionate,
then certainly those who love God should be
compassionate as well.
The God whom Jesus announces
and in whose name he acts is the God of
compassion,
the God who offers himself
as example and model for all human behavior.

(HN, *The Return of the Prodigal Son*)

Silent Reflection

The Canticle of Zachary

> God be blessed!
> I now am free, because I belong to God...

Prayers of Gratitude

The Lord's Prayer

Sharing of the Peace / The Sign of the Cross

> May God bless us, free us from all harm,
> and lead us to life everlasting. Amen.

WEEK THREE

If prayer leads us
into a deeper unity with the compassionate Christ,
it will always give rise
to concrete acts of service.
And if concrete acts of service
do indeed lead us
to a deeper solidarity with the poor,
the hungry, the sick,
the dying, and the oppressed,
then they will always give rise to prayer.

(HN, *Compassion: A Reflection on the Christian Life*)

Sunday Evening Prayer I

Invitatory / The Sign of the Cross

Optional Song or Hymn

Psalm 113:6–9

> *From east to west—praise God!*

> Our God bends low
>> to see both heaven and earth—
>> to raise up the weak from the dust
>> and to lift the poor from the ash heap,
>> seating them in the company of princes,
>> yes, with royalty and empire.

> The childless are no longer alone,
>> rejoicing now with many children.

(DH, adapt.)

Pause for Silent Prayer

Psalm 116:10–19

> *I will raise high the cup of liberation*
> *and call upon the name of God.*

> Yes, I am afflicted—yet I still believe.
> Yes, I am battered with lies—yet I still believe.

> How can I possibly find a way
>> to return to God
>> the astonishing gift that I have been given?

I will raise the cup of liberation
and sing the name of God!
I will keep my vows to you, God,
and I will do so before your people.

God, you shed your own tears
when death comes to those
who have been faithful to you.
I beg you, God, hear me.
Here I am, your servant whom you love.
You have freed me from death.

My entire life will be a gift
of thanksgiving to you
as I call upon you, as I proclaim your name.
I will keep my vows to you, God,
and I will do so before your people—
in your house,
in the heart of your Jerusalem.

(DH, adapt.)

From Henri

As long as we belong to this world,
we will remain subject to its competitive ways
and expect to be rewarded for all the good we do.
But when we belong to God,
who loves us without conditions,
we can live as he does.
The great conversion called for by Jesus

is to move from belonging to the world
to belonging to God.

(HN, *The Return of the Prodigal Son*)

Silent Reflection

The Canticle of Mary

My soul is bursting with how great God is!
My spirit cannot stop rejoicing ...

Prayers of Intercession

The Lord's Prayer

Sharing of the Peace / The Sign of the Cross

May God bless us, free us from all harm,
and lead us to life everlasting. Amen.

Sunday Morning Prayer

Invitatory / The Sign of the Cross

Optional Song or Hymn

Psalm 93

> *High above the waves,*
> *God rises above all with power.*
>
> God is in charge.
> God reigns.
>
> God's robes cover
> the earth with goodness
> and strength.
>
> The vast cloth of God
> is a gift
> wrapping with power -
> and the world watches firmly,
> not afraid,
> not shaken,
> but welcoming and opened
> for God's direction,
> a most ageless path.
>
> Onward roll the tides
> and the surging waves -
> like the crack of thunder,
> relentless,
> intense,
> unrelenting.

Energy!

Sailing and crackling
    above the waters,
    higher than the breakers -
    God rising,
    God who is mighty,
    God who rules.

God's commands are eternal
    and cannot be brought down.
Holiness is everywhere,
    holiness enlightening!

(DH, adapt.)

Pause for Silent Prayer

Psalm 148

*From the heights and from the depths,
sing praise!*

Praise God with beauty unspeakable!
Praise God from the crown of the mountain!
All angels, praise!
All heavenly hosts, praise!

The brightness of the sun,
    the brilliance of the moon,
    the sparkle of the stars,
    the splash of the rain,
    the thrill of heaven,
    the heat of the fire,
    the depths of the depths,
    the creatures that crawl and swim,
    the rush of the waters -
    all offer up your praise!

All people, royal and common!
All who judge and all who follow!

Women and men,
    young and old,
      offer up the name in praise -
      the name that drowns out
      all other names!

Beyond words praise be given!
All that is life - praise!
All that is and can be created - praise!
From our yesterdays through our tomorrows,
    may all laws be celebrated inside and outside!

God's people be strong!
God's faithful shout praise!
Rise up all children of Israel -
    all sing and be praise!

(DH, adapt.)

From Henri

The mystery of the spiritual life
is that Jesus desires to meet us
in the seclusion of our own heart,
to make his love known to us there,
to free us from our fears,
and to make our own deepest self known to us.
In the privacy of our heart, therefore,
we can learn not only to know Jesus but,
through Jesus, ourselves as well.

(*Letters to Marc About Jesus: Living a Spiritual Life in a Material World*)

Silent Reflection

The Canticle of Zachary

> God be blessed!
> I now am free, because I belong to God ...

Prayers of Gratitude

The Lord's Prayer

Sharing of the Peace / The Sign of the Cross

> May God bless us, free us from all harm,
> and lead us to life everlasting. Amen.

Sunday Evening Prayer II

Invitatory / The Sign of the Cross

Optional Song or Hymn

Psalm 110:1, 3–4

> *God cries out to all who rule:*
> *Sit at my right hand.*
>
> For all of us who dare to lead,
>> we need to remember
>> that any power that we have
>> is grounded in God's covenant.
>
> Only then,
>> will we have the loyalty of the people.
>
> If we remember this,
>> then the people will be one with us,
>> and stand with us.
> Then our power is truly holy,
>> renewed and fresh,
>> and born again like the dawn.
>
> God gives us this most blessed oath:
>
> "You are my servant, forever;
>> because I have made it so."

(DH, adapt.)

Pause for Silent Prayer

Psalm 111

Who can ignore and forget the wonder of God?
God is kind and merciful.

Not half way,
    not mere lip service -
    but with the entirety
    and fullness of my heart
    I want to,   I must,   praise the God of justice.

Digging deep,
    I know that God's actions
    are a delight for my heart:
    for God's justice is real,
    sturdy,
    dependable.

Who could ever forget?
This God,
    kind and merciful,
    nourishing always,
    keeping promises,
    manifesting glory
    and making the land fruitful.

God's commands
    are full of truth.
God's commands
    are brimming with justice.
God's commands
    are to be trusted.

Forever.

We are holy by God's hand,
    and faithfulness

is the result of God's actions!
God's name must be honored.
God's name must be given praise.
If we truly seek wisdom,
we will see God.

Give Praise!

(DH, adapt.)

From Henri

Each time you let the love of God
penetrate deeper into your heart,
you lose a bit of your anxiety,
and overtime you shed a bit of your anxiety,
you learn to know yourself better
and long all the more to be known by your loving
God.
Thus, the more you learn to love God,
the more you learn to know and cherish yourself.

(*Letters to Marc About Jesus: Living a Spiritual Life in a
Material World*)

Silent Reflection

The Canticle of Mary

My soul is bursting with how great God is!
My spirit cannot stop rejoicing …

Prayers of Intercession

The Lord's Prayer

Sharing of the Peace / The Sign of the Cross

May God bless us, free us from all harm,
and lead us to life everlasting. Amen.

Monday Morning Prayer

Invitatory / The Sign of the Cross

Optional Song or Hymn

Psalm 84:2–6, 9–13

> *What a joy to live with you,*
> *God of the glory of heaven.*

Your home.
Where you live.
Beautiful.
I ache to be there.

My whole heart,
    my entire body,   sings –
    sings to you,   my living God.

Even the smallest of birds
    find a place for a home,
    a space
    to land, to settle.

They can open up
    and serve their young
    at your table of life;
    your heavenly regiment
    serves -
    my God.

My dear God.

To live and linger with you
    is such a blessing;
    a most precious joy
    that goes on forever and ever.

To hold the courage
    that you provide
    settles our hearts
    to make the journey.

One moment with you -
    a single instant -
    is so much more
    than thousands deprived.

I long to settle at your door
    rather then to move among those
    who bring fear and wrong and hurt.

Sun.
Guide and guard.
Grace and honor - given.
Never holding back
    generously blessing
    those who live in the right.

You and your holy sentinels
    are most sacred indeed -
    and given due loyalty
    from all who place in you their trust.

Security.
You.

(DH, adapt.)

Pause for Silent Prayer

Psalm 96:1–6, 11–13

> *Make music, blessing God's name,*
> *daily make praise!*

Join me
        and join this most blessed earth
        in singing a new song to God:
        a new melody
        with fresh and daring harmonies
        growing and blooming
        and bursting,
        singing and praising God's name!

Bring with you
        a daily portion of phrases
        and rhythms
        that save!
Sing this song everywhere,
        sharing God's miracles,
        proclaiming God's wonders!

God is awesome and great –
        sing about that!
God is honored
        by our tremendous displays
        of power –
        for it is God alone who designed the heavens,
        who had sight put on the stars,
        and who marked the night with light!

Everyone, listen!
Recognize this light!
Bathe your faces in its blinding brilliance!
Place yourself in the center of it all
    and recognize what a gift it is!

Then the trees throughout all creation
    will brim strong with dignity –
    greening more and more
    with praise to this God
    who is coming,
    coming to bloom with justice;
    coming to take hold of this world,
    and infuse our hearts
    with the sweet gift of truth.

(DH, adapt.)

From Henri

My broader vocation
is simply to enjoy God's presence,
do God's will,
and be grateful wherever I am.
The question of where to live and what to do
is really insignificant compared to the question
of how to keep the eyes of my heart
focused on the Lord.

(*Discernment: Reading the Signs of Daily Life*)

Silent Reflection

The Canticle of Zachary

God be blessed!
I now am free, because I belong to God ...

Prayers of Gratitude

The Lord's Prayer

Sharing of the Peace / The Sign of the Cross

>May God bless us, free us from all harm,
>and lead us to life everlasting. Amen.

Monday Evening Prayer

Invitatory / The Sign of the Cross

Optional Song or Hymn

Psalm 123

> *Our eyes are resting on you, God,*
> *patiently awaiting your mercy.*

Our eyes sink into your presence,
　　totally fixed on you.

Our eyes want to stay on you,
　　gaze on you,
　　always seeking you,
　　searching you,
　　longing for you.

Our eyes are so focused on you,
　　like a slave following their master,
　　like a servant loyal to her mistress;
　　we will not deter from you,
　　we are waiting for your mercy.

Keep showing your mercy to us,
　　for we have suffered so much,
　　and we are desperate for relief
　　from the mockery we receive;
　　and from the shame
　　that is thrust upon us.

(DH, adapt.)

Pause for Silent Prayer

Psalm 124

God, the creator of earth and sky,
is our help, protecting us.

We are now, souls - rescued,
　　like a bird fleeing the hunter.

If God had not stayed with us,
　　If God had not been with us and for us –
　　then we would have been eaten alive,
　　destroyed by the heat, anger and rage
　　of those who hate us.

We would have drowned
　　from the waters in their tempest,
　　the surge of the waves
　　would have consumed us,
　　overwhelmed us.

But God came
　　and broke open the trapper's net –
　　the snare is broken.
We are set free.

God is our help –
　　the creator the earth and sky.

(DH, adapt.)

From Henri

Healing means moving from your pain to the pain.
When you keep focusing

on the specific circumstances of your pain,
you easily become angry, resentful, and even
vindictive.
You are inclined to do something about the
externals of your pain
in order to relieve it;
this explains why you often seek revenge.
But real healing comes from realizing
that your own particularly pain is a share in
humanity's pain.
That realization allows you to forgive your enemies
and enter into a truly compassionate way of life.
That is the way of Jesus.

*(The Inner Voice of Love: A Journey through
Anguish to Freedom)*

Silent Reflection

The Canticle of Mary

My soul is bursting with how great God is!
My spirit cannot stop rejoicing ...

Prayers of Intercession

The Lord's Prayer

Sharing of the Peace / The Sign of the Cross

May God bless us, free us from all harm,
and lead us to life everlasting. Amen.

Tuesday Morning Prayer

Invitatory / The Sign of the Cross

Optional Song or Hymn

Psalm 85

> *Justice is the path of God,*
> *always pointing the way.*

God,
> you look kindly
> upon our parched land;
> upon our dusty hearts.

Forgiving shame,
> cleansing us of all fault,
> controlling rage,
> shunning anger.

Come to us,
> but not in anger or fury!
Come to us,
> with grace and tenderness.

Pierce our dryness
> and bring forth lives that blossom.
Breathe life into your people,
> your "no longer abandoned"
> and cover us with your joy!

Forgive.

Restore.

Come and revive.
Draw near and nourish.
Come close.
Show mercy.

Open up love.

I will take a moment.
Stop.
I will listen to what God is saying to me,
    right here, right now.

God is speaking that we might listen:

Peace.

Peace to all people –
    to those who keep faith
    and for all who lean their hearts
    toward God.

We can be saved from our terror,
    if we would only honor God
    and what God honors –
    then glory can
    and will
    dwell among us.

True mercy, love
and faithfulness are real.
Justice and peace have embraced
and their relationship is sealed.

Fused together - cauterized.
Unbreakable.

Faith is bursting forth from the earth,
and all that is just is hovering over us,
providing a canopy of protection.

God will keep blessing us,
and all living things on this earth
will welcome in this blessing,
with justice leading the way
guiding the way of God
to interrupt our ways.

(DH, adapt.)

Pause for Silent Prayer

Psalm 67

God, show us your face.
Make yourself known to us.

Care for us.
Bless us.
Shine your face upon us.
Reveal yourself to us.
Bear life in us.
Bring out praise in us.

Let all the earth know

how you keep breathing in us;
how you continually
guide all creation –
everyone, everything
follows you
to your destination,
your land of justice,
your resting place of honor.

The richness of the land
    sprouts forth the harvest –
O God,
    how you have blest us!

Do not relent –
    keep the blessings coming!
And may we all
    embrace and make known
    our prayer of praise -
    our worship to you.

(DH, adapt.)

From Henri

There is no such thing as the right place or the right job.
I can be miserable or joyful,
restless or at peace, in all situations ...
I have no lasting dwelling on this earth ...
I am a traveler on the way to a sacred place
where God holds me in the palm of his hand.
This deeper awareness sets me free
to be a pilgrim,
to pray without ceasing,
and to be grateful.

(Discernment: Reading the Signs of Daily Life)

Silent Reflection

The Canticle of Zachary

> God be blessed!
> I now am free, because I belong to God ...

Prayers of Gratitude

The Lord's Prayer

Sharing of the Peace / The Sign of the Cross

> May God bless us, free us from all harm,
> and lead us to life everlasting. Amen.

Tuesday Evening Prayer

Invitatory / The Sign of the Cross

Optional Song or Hymn

Psalm 125

> *Just as the mountains embrace Jerusalem,*
> *so does God embrace us.*

Let go.

Trust in God,
    and be like Zion -
      strong, unmovable, enduring.

Just as the mountains surround us,
    let God embrace you
    day after day,
    from tomorrow to tomorrow.

Unending.
Let God ring you in.

Keep close to the border of righteousness.
Keep wrong choices
    and misguided directions at bay.
It get's slippery.

So God,
    bring your goodness
    to the good ones.
Bring your justice
    to the just ones.

Bring your truth
    to the ones whose hearts are true.
The cruel and the evil
    will continue to bring their poison.
Cast these powers away!

Give us peace.
A peace that lasts.

(DH, adapt.)

Pause for Silent Prayer

Psalm 131

Every part of me rests in you, God.

You: peace.

Not haughty,
    not arrogant,
    not reaching beyond myself.

You: peace.

But yes, calm.
Still.
Like a child
    sinking -
    surrendering to mother.

Rest.

You: peace.

Everyone,
    wait for God.

Always.

You: peace.

(DH, adapt.)

From Henri

> In the act of prayer,
> we undermine the illusion of control
> by divesting ourselves of all false belongings
> and by directing ourselves totally
> to the God who is the only one to whom we belong.
> Prayer, therefore,
> is the act of dying to all that we consider to be our
> own
> and of being born to a new existence
> which is not of this world.
> Prayer is indeed a death to the world
> so we can live for God.

(Peacework: Prayer, Resistance, Community)

Silent Reflection

The Canticle of Mary

> My soul is bursting with how great God is!
> My spirit cannot stop rejoicing ...

Prayers of Intercession

The Lord's Prayer

Sharing of the Peace / The Sign of the Cross

> May God bless us, free us from all harm,
> and lead us to life everlasting. Amen.

Wednesday Morning Prayer

Invitatory / The Sign of the Cross

Optional Song or Hymn

Psalm 86

>*I surrender myself to you, God.*
>*Lavish me with joy as I serve you.*

>I am clinging on to a final hope.
>That hope is you.
>I am nearly completely broken.

>My faith is fragile,
>>my trust is weak, my life is vulnerable,
>>but my faith in you remains.

>Give me courage, God.
>I need you so much
>>and I am crying out constantly.
>Refresh my soul,
>>as I give my life over to you.

>You are good.
>You are pardon, healing and grace.
>Please come quickly,
>>take on my life
>>and drown me with your mercy.
>Hear my voice - listen to me.

>I know as much as I know anything
>>that you will catch me in my falling.

You will heal me in my fearful state,
  because you are my amazing miracle:
  the hope
  that I have been searching for to believe in.

Nothing,
  no one - can even barely come as close as you,
  in entering into the mix of my dreams;
  lifting me up to believe in them.

Because it is you
  who opens and strengthens my weary eyes
  to really see with a fresh clarity -
  as though for the very first time -
  that such dreams are not to be laughed at,
  but rather,
  embraced as storylines
  that can and do come true.

(DH, adapt.)

Pause for Silent Prayer

Psalm 98:2–3

Blow the trumpets,
Shout to God, our sovereign.

God:
Victory is made known.
Justice is revealed.
Mercy,

blessed mercy -
is never forgotten;
it is ever loyal.

Always faithful.

(DH, adapt.)

From Henri

Living a spiritually mature life
requires listening to God's voice within and among us.
Our God is a God who cares, heals,
guides, directs, challenges, confronts, corrects.
To discern means first of all to listen to God,
to pay attention to God's active presence,
and to obey God's prompting, direction,
leadings, and guidance.

(Discernment: Reading the Signs of Daily Life)

Silent Reflection

The Canticle of Zachary

God be blessed!
I now am free, because I belong to God ...

Prayers of Gratitude

The Lord's Prayer

Sharing of the Peace / The Sign of the Cross

May God bless us, free us from all harm,
and lead us to life everlasting. Amen.

Wednesday Evening Prayer

Invitatory / The Sign of the Cross

Optional Song or Hymn

Psalm 126

> *Singing, dancing, laughing -*
> *God's destiny for all who weep.*

You bring us out of our cell,
    our "locked in" place.

The dreaming is now set free!
Laughter now replaces our tears!
Dancing arrives to our crippled legs!
Songs return to our silent lips!

Others now say:

"Yes!
    Look at them!
    God is with them!
    Wonderful things are happening
    to them who have struggled -
    God is the reason!
    Rejoice in this!"

God,
    share with us the same drink
    that they are consuming -
    we too, thirst -
    we ache to be drunk with the water
    that can cover the dry ground.

May our tears
> be the fountain that nurtures
> and brings back
> singing, dancing, and laughing.

They once left weeping and grieving,
> and they planted the seed.
Now, they come back -
> and we want to join them
> in their song, dance and joy!

(DH, adapt.)

Pause for Silent Prayer

Psalm 127

> *God builds the house and watches over us.*

If God is not the one
> building my house,
> the work will be useless –
> it will fall.
> If God is not keeping watch,
> those who stand guard -
> will watch and standby in vain.

If we rise early
> and work and sweat all day for bread,
> we are foolish.
If God is pleased,
> we will all receive,
> even when we are at rest.

Children are a most blessed gift from God,
> and a precious blessing
> for those who bear them.
They are like the arrows of the archer.

So very happy and grateful
are those whose quiver is full –
they will bear no reason to be ashamed
when facing their foes.

(DH, adapt.)

From Henri

In solitude I get rid of my scaffolding:
no friends to talk with, no telephone calls to make,
no meetings to attend, no music to entertain,
no books to distract, just me -
naked, vulnerable, weak, sinful, deprived, broken -
nothing.
It is this nothingness that I have to face in my
solitude,
a nothingness so dreadful that everything in me
wants to run to my friends, my work, and my
distractions
so that I can forget my nothingness
and make myself believe that I am worth
something.

*(The Way of the Heart: Connecting with God through
Prayer, Wisdom, and Silence)*

Silent Reflection

The Canticle of Mary

My soul is bursting with how great God is!
My spirit cannot stop rejoicing …

Prayers of Intercession

The Lord's Prayer

Sharing of the Peace / The Sign of the Cross

May God bless us, free us from all harm,
and lead us to life everlasting. Amen.

Thursday Morning Prayer

Invitatory / The Sign of the Cross

Optional Song or Hymn

Psalm 87

> *Great is the city of God.*
>
> We all have our "Zion's" –
>   our holy mountains
>   that are created by God,
>   that greatly surpass
>   all other places
>   in own Israel,
>   of our own home.
>
> Glorious things happen
>   and are spoken at these places.
>
> These are places of wholeness.
>
> Birth.
>
> Born from these "Zion's."
> And God sustains this wholeness;
>   guides and protects.
>
> God knows our names,
>   and keeps a record of our birth
>   and rebirth.

Such wonder we have seen,
    and so we sing and dance
    our way home.

(DH, adapt.)

Pause for Silent Prayer

Psalm 99:1–3

Bow down. Worship God.
Offer your praise in this glorious house.

Even though
    we are sometimes lured
    into thinking we are –
    the truth is
    that we are not God!

We are not in charge:
God is.

God reigns.
When God speaks
    all creation responds:
    with trembling and shaking.

It is not so much that we are good,
    that drives us to celebrate.

Rather,
    it is because of the blessed fact
    that God is good.

(DH, adapt.)

From Henri

Are we willing to spend time with those
who do not stimulate our curiosity?
Do we listen to those who do not immediately
attract us?
Can we be compassionate to those
whose suffering remains hidden from the eyes of
the world?
There is much hidden suffering ...
Once we look downward
instead of upward on the ladder of life,
we see see the pain of people wherever we go,
and we hear the call of compassion wherever we are.
True compassion always begins right where we are.

(Here and Now: Living in the Spirit)

Silent Reflection

The Canticle of Zachary

God be blessed!
I now am free, because I belong to God ...

Prayers of Gratitude

The Lord's Prayer

Sharing of the Peace / The Sign of the Cross

May God bless us, free us from all harm,
and lead us to life everlasting. Amen.

Thursday Evening Prayer

Invitatory / The Sign of the Cross

Optional Song or Hymn

Psalm 55:2–15

> *You, God,*
> *alone are my dearest and most treasured*
> *companion.*

> Listen to me,
>   I beg you, do not ignore me.
> I am shaking,
>   and terrified.

> My heart - racing.
> I can feel, touch and sense
>   death coming near.
> I am trembling.

> "If only I had the wings of a dove -
>   for if I did
>   I would fly as far away as I could
>   to the wilderness
>   to be protected from the brimming storm."

> I ask you:
>   stir up confusion and blur the rage,
>   for I see too much violence and hardship
>   lurking about this space
>   throughout the day and night.

Oppression, deception,
    destruction and lies
    surround,
    never leaving.

But with you,
    I can withstand the insults
    and survive all plots
    to do me harm.

Why?

Because you are my friend,
    the one whom I know so well.
Always in conversation
    with each other;
    you keep walking by my side,
    especially in dark times.

You -
    my dearest
    and most trusted companion.

(DH, adapt.)

Pause for Silent Prayer

Psalm 132:13–18

    The poor will be fed. Bless Zion!

God has chosen Zion.
God has chosen all of us
    and desires us
    to have this sacred home.

God has chosen our hearts
　　for this home,
　　an everlasting dwelling place.

This home
　　will be blessed with abundance –
　　especially for the poor.
All who serve
　　will be cloaked in holiness,
　　and the faithful
　　will end up singing and singing!

This home
　　is the center of strength
　　for the power of light
　　　for God's anointed.
Those who oppose this gift,
　　will be covered in shame.
But God's anointed
　　will receive a crown bearing light!

(DH, adapt.)

From Henri

As soon as I decide to stay in my solitude,
confusing ideas, disturbing images, wild fantasies,
and weird associations jump about in my mind
like monkeys in a banana tree ...
The task is to persevere in my solitude,
to stay in my cell until all my seductive visitors
get tired of pounding on my door and leave me alone.

*(The Way of the Heart: Connecting with God through
Prayer, Wisdom, and Silence)*

Silent Reflection

The Canticle of Mary

> My soul is bursting with how great God is!
> My spirit cannot stop rejoicing ...

Prayers of Intercession

The Lord's Prayer

Sharing of the Peace / The Sign of the Cross

> May God bless us, free us from all harm,
> and lead us to life everlasting. Amen.

Friday Morning Prayer

Invitatory / The Sign of the Cross

Optional Song or Hymn

Psalm 51

> *Have mercy on us, and share your mercy.*

Make clean and clear away
    all of the dust and debris
    from my heart.
Come and bring a steadiness,
    a smooth path to my spirit.
Do not abandon me -
    hold me tightly to your presence.

Help me,
    convince me
    that joy will follow pain.

Sustain and support me;
    and know
    that I will provide the direction
    to those who need
    to return to you.

Stop the tears
    so I will be able to sing a song
    love-packed with the taste of you.

Provide for my voice
    to clearly become a shout
    of praise to you.

Courage.
Bring courage to my heart.

Sacrifices will not work.
They do not satisfy you.
So then,
    I offer you my broken self:
    my fragile heart,
    my tender spirit.

These things you welcome.

You will not turn away,
    because you have my heart.

(DH, adapt.)

Pause for Silent Prayer

Psalm 100

God shepherds us - we, the flock.

Break through!
Shout out, all the earth!

Serve!

With glad hearts -
    approach God and sing!

It is God - yes!
It is God who made us.

We belong to God;
  we are the flock who follows!

Come enter through the door
  with everlasting thanksgiving.

Come in, everyone,
  with singing to the name of God:
  Holy! Give thanks!

God's goodness never ends,
  and is faithful always.
From the beginning of life
  through the life after life,
  no one can put a stop
  to God's goodness,
  God's mercy,
  God's amazing love!

(DH, adapt.)

From Henri

The great spiritual call of the Beloved of God
is to pull their brokenness away
from the shadow of the curse
and put it under the light of the blessing ...
the great task becomes that of allowing the blessing
to touch us in our brokenness.
Then our brokenness will gradually come to be seen
as an opening toward the full acceptance
of ourselves as the Beloved.

(Life of the Beloved)

Silent Reflection

The Canticle of Zachary

> God be blessed!
> I now am free, because I belong to God ...

Prayers of Gratitude

The Lord's Prayer

Sharing of the Peace / The Sign of the Cross

> May God bless us, free us from all harm,
> and lead us to life everlasting. Amen.

Friday Evening Prayer

Invitatory / The Sign of the Cross

Optional Song or Hymn

Psalm 135:1–7

> *Make music, sing hymns - for God is good.*
> *Delight in God.*

Alleluia!

Give praise to the name of God,
   give praise,
   give praise,
   keep on giving praise!

All of you who have a servant's heart –
   give praise!

All of you who stand in God's presence –
   give praise!

All of you who long to sing
   a hymn of thanksgiving to God –
   give praise!

Israel, every nation –
   give praise!

God is great indeed,
   and surpasses every gift
   over and over again.

If God wants it so –
    it will be so!
No matter what,
    and no matter where:
    in heaven,
    on the earth,
    or in the sea.

God adorns the earth with clouds,
    and never hesitates
    to burst forth lightning for the rain,
    or to release the brilliant breath of life!

(DH, adapt.)

Pause for Silent Prayer

Psalm 135:13–21

Israel! Bless God!
Sing!

Your name is relentless - it is forever.
Your glory never fades - it is forever.
You are justice for your people
and you are attentive to their needs.

The things of gold and silver
are the idols of human hands.
Their mouths cannot make a sound.
Their eyes see nothing.
Their ears cannot hear anything.
Their nostrils cannot find air to breathe.

Israel - bless God!
House of Aaron,
House of Levi - bless God!
All who are faithful - bless God!

> Bless the God of Zion,
> who calls Jerusalem home.

(DH, adapt.)

From Henri

> The world is evil only when you become its slave.
> The world has a lot to offer -
> just as Egypt did for the children of Jacob -
> as long as you don't feel bound to obey it.
> The great struggle facing you
> is not to leave the world,
> to reject your ambition and aspirations,
> or to despise money, prestige, or success,
> but to claim your spiritual truth
> and to live in the world
> as someone who doesn't belong to it.

(*Life of the Beloved*)

Silent Reflection

The Canticle of Mary

> My soul is bursting with how great God is!
> My spirit cannot stop rejoicing ...

Prayers of Intercession

The Lord's Prayer

Sharing of the Peace / The Sign of the Cross

> May God bless us, free us from all harm,
> and lead us to life everlasting. Amen.

Saturday Morning Prayer

Invitatory / Sign of the Peace

Optional Song or Hymn

Psalm 119:145–152

> *Your law, O God, is the only truth I need.*

With a heart so full,
   I ache for you to hear me.
Bring the freedom I seek
   so I may follow you.

I have turned my face to you
   during the cold of the night,
   waiting,
   praying,
   to hear from you.

Throughout the night I have kept vigil,
   lingering,
   pondering,
   musing upon your promises.

Listen to me,
   you, the "God who loves;"
   may I live by your justice.
Those who want to cause harm
   are closing in.

But you, God,
   you even closer, so very close.

Your way shines with truth!

Since I was young
> I have learned these things about you,
> and they are rooted in me forever.

(DH, adapt.)

Pause for Silent Prayer

Psalm 117

> *Strong is the love of God.*
> *Faithful is God.*

> Praise!
> From every land,
> > from every throat,
> > from the deepest heart,
> > from all people -
> > praise!

> And yes, glory!
> Glory to God!

> The love is so strong,
> > so embracing,
> > so faithful.

> Without end.
> Infinite.

> Now, praise that!

(DH, adapt.)

From Henri

> Our humanity comes to its fullest bloom in giving.
> We become beautiful people
> when we give whatever we can give:
> a smile, a handshake, a kiss, an embrace,
> a word of love, a present, a part of our life ...
> all of our life.
> How true it is
> that our lives find their fulfillment
> in giving ourselves to others.
>
> *(Life of the Beloved)*

Silent Reflection

The Canticle of Zachary

> God be blessed!
> I now am free, because I belong to God ...

Prayers of Gratitude

The Lord's Prayer

Sharing of the Peace / The Sign of the Cross

> May God bless us, free us from all harm,
> and lead us to life everlasting. Amen.

WEEK FOUR

To pray, that is,
to listen to the voice
of the One who calls us the "beloved,"
is to learn that this voice excludes no one.
Where I dwell,
God dwells with me,
and where God dwells within me
I find all my sisters and brothers.

(*Here and Now: Living in the Spirit*)

Sunday Evening Prayer I

Invitatory / The Sign of the Cross

Optional Song or Hymn

Psalm 122

> *Sing joyfully:*
> *"Let us go to God's house!"*

I heard them say with boundless joy,
"Let us go to God's house!"
Jerusalem - we are here inside your gates.

Jerusalem is set so perfectly
that the city and the temple are one.
It is to you, Jerusalem,
that every tribe ascends.

We are commanded to honor the name of God.
The places of righteousness and justice are here,
in line with the glory of David.

For Jerusalem - pray for peace.
For Jerusalem - pray for happiness in every home.
For Jerusalem - pray for safety in their walls.
For Jerusalem - pray for peace in every dwelling.

For love of my family and friends
let me sing, "Peace!"

For love of God's own house,
I pledge myself

and pray seeking goodness -
for you.

(DH, adapt.)

Pause for Silent Prayer

Psalm 130

From morning to nighttime,
we wait for God.

Right now,
    at this very moment –
I feel so empty.
I need to grab on to something,
    I need to know
    that you are not cutting me off.
I need to know that you are listening.
Hear me!

I am begging you,
    please have mercy on me,
    because if you were to keep count
    of all my sins,
    of all my horrible deeds,
    I would not be able to survive
    your judgment.

But you do forgive.
You keep on forgiving me.
I trust in that –
I trust in you.
I wait and keep watch for you.

I am one with everyone
who is waiting for you.
I will wait
and I know you will fill me
with grace,
with mercy -
and I will be free from my sin.

(DH, adapt.)

From Henri

When we are spiritually deaf,
we are not aware that anything important
is happening in our lives.
We keep running away from the present moment,
and we try to create experiences
that make our lives worthwhile.
So we fill up our time to avoid the emptiness
we otherwise would feel.
When we are truly listening,
we come to know that God is speaking to us,
pointing the way, showing the direction.

(*Discernment: Reading the Signs of Daily Life*)

Silent Reflection

The Canticle of Mary

My soul is bursting with how great God is!
My spirit cannot stop rejoicing ...

Prayers of Intercession

The Lord's Prayer

Sharing of the Peace / The Sign of the Cross

May God bless us, free us from all harm,
and lead us to life everlasting. Amen.

Sunday Morning Prayer

Invitatory / The Sign of the Cross

Optional Song or Hymn

Psalm 118:1–4, 10–14

> *This is God's day.*
> *Rejoice! Be glad!*

Praise and unending thanksgiving
    be to you:
        For your mercy pierces through!

Let all who struggle and suffer,
    speak and celebrate:
        For your mercy pierces through!

Let the house of Aaron,
    and every house,
        speak and celebrate:
            For your mercy pierces through!

Let all who honor your name,
    speak and celebrate:
        For your mercy pierces through!

The nations from every corner
    engulf and attempt to swallow me:
        But by your name, I cut them off!

They surround me like bees
    threatening to sting:
        But by your name, I cut them off!

They plot to blaze up
>   a thorn-filled fire:
>   But by your name, I cut them off!

They thrust into me
>   deeply and with the intent of death.
But you,
>   you protect me.

You are my song
>   that keeps me strong.
You are my song
>   of compassion and rescue.

(DH, adapt.)

Pause for Silent Prayer

Psalm 150

Everything that is living and moving -
Praise God!

You!

Praise You!
You in your home!
You in the heavens!

You!

Strong!
Holy!
Deeds upon deeds!

You!

Power from the trumpets!
Glory from the many strings!

Harps with glissandos!
Justice dancing!
Drums pounding!
Timbrel clanging!
Pipes blasting!

You!

Joy from crashing cymbals!
Ecstasy from ringing!
Endless bell overtones!
Everything resonating!
Everything breathing fully and clearly!
Everything alive!

You!

(DH, adapt.)

From Henri

Everything changes radically
from the moment you know yourself
as being sent into the world.
The change of which I speak is the change
from living life as a painful test to prove
that you deserve to be loved,
to living it as an unceasing "Yes"
to the truth of that Belovedness.
Put simply, life is a God-given opportunity
to become who we are,
to affirm our own spiritual nature,
claim the truth,
appropriate and integrate the reality of our being,
but, most of all,
to say "Yes" to the One who calls us the Beloved.

(*Life of the Beloved*)

Silent Reflection

The Canticle of Zachary

> God be blessed!
> I now am free, because I belong to God ...

Prayers of Gratitude

The Lord's Prayer

Sharing of the Peace / The Sign of the Cross

> May God bless us, free us from all harm,
> and lead us to life everlasting. Amen.

Sunday Evening Prayer II

Invitatory / The Sign of the Cross

Optional Song or Hymn

Psalm 110:1, 3–4

> *Born anew, like the rising sun.*
> *Fresh as the dew.*

> For all of us who dare to lead,
>> we need to remember
>> that any power that we have
>> is grounded in God's covenant.

> Only then,
>> will we have the loyalty of the people.

> If we remember this,
>> then the people will be one with us,
>> and stand with us.
> Then our power is truly holy,
>> renewed and fresh,
>> and born again like the dawn.

> God gives us this most blessed oath:

> "You are my servant, forever;
>> because I have made it so."

(DH, adapt.)

Pause for Silent Prayer

Psalm 112:1b–2, 4–5, 9

God is justice and mercy.
We who love God - happy and blessed are we.

If you seek holiness,
    love God fiercely.
For then,
    you will have children blest,
    strong and grace-filled.

The sun will dawn on you,
    with light shining,
    blinding darkness,
    with mercy and justice breaking through.

Charity and generosity
    will be found everywhere,
    fairness, integrity.

Remembered.
Yes.

Trusting in God will be
    buoyant and free,
    yet steady and filled with courage.
Enemies shrink:
    good news - only good news.

The poor are lifted high;
    righteousness prevails.
Honor discovered,
    nurtured,
    sustained.

Glory!

(DH, adapt.)

From Henri

When life seems harried
and continues to have hard moments,
we can believe that something good
is happening amid all of this.
We get glimpses of how God
might be working out his purposes in our days.
Time becomes not just something to get through
or manipulate of mange,
but the arena of God's good work in us.
Whatever happens - good things or bad,
pleasant or problematic -
we ask,
"What might God be doing here?"
We see the events of the day
as continuous occasions to change the heart.

(Discernment: Reading the Signs of Daily Life)

Silent Reflection

The Canticle of Mary

My soul is bursting with how great God is!
My spirit cannot stop rejoicing ...

Prayers of Intercession

The Lord's Prayer

Sharing of the Peace / The Sign of the Cross

May God bless us, free us from all harm,
and lead us to life everlasting. Amen.

Monday Morning Prayer

Invitatory / The Sign of the Cross

Optional Song or Hymn

Psalm 90:1–2, 4, 13–17

> *Let your love shine on us in the morning,*
> *bringing gladness to our days.*

Come back.

You keep things steady.
We hold on to you
    from forever to forever.

Before there were mountains,
    there was you.
Before any beginning,
    middle or end, there was you.
You have always been
    our God, forever -
    before any beginnings were imagined.

You.

Come back.

Time is lost on you.
Your eyes are like a thousand years
    that have come and gone over and over
    without any beginning or ending.
Time has come and gone -

night and day like yesterday,
and again - gone.

Come back.

Why must we wait?
How long are we to endure?
Why are our days numbered?
Come back.
Soon.

Fill us at dawn,
    fill us as fully as you can
    with a love and energy
    that can transform our pain
    and bless us with joy,
    making us whole again.

Come back.

All need to know -
all of us who serve you,
the old and the young.
Let your love shine all over us -
on our work, bring success;
all of our work for ourselves,
each other - and You.

Come back.

(DH, adapt.)

Psalm 135:1–7, 19–21

> *Praise the name of God,*
> *all you who serve God.*

Alleluia!

Give praise to the name of God,
    give praise,
    give praise,
    keep on giving praise!

All of you who have a servant's heart –
    give praise!

All of you who stand in God's presence –
    give praise!

All of you who long to sing
    a hymn of thanksgiving to God –
    give praise!

Israel, every nation –
    give praise!

God is great indeed,
    and surpasses every gift
    over and over again.

If God wants it so –
    it will be so!
No matter what,
    and no matter where:
    in heaven,

on the earth,
or in the sea.

God adorns the earth with clouds,
and never hesitates
to burst forth lightning for the rain,
or to release the brilliant breath of life!

May every home give praise!

Alleluia!

(DH, adapt.)

From Henri

God's forgiveness is unconditional;
it comes from a heart
that does not demand anything for itself,
a heart that is completely empty of self-seeking.
It is this divine forgiveness
that I have to practice in my daily life.
It calls me to keep stepping over all my arguments
that say forgiveness is unwise, unhealthy, and
impractical.
It challenges me to step over all my needs
for gratitude and compliments.
Finally, it demands of me
that I step over the wounded part of my heart
that feels hurt and wronged and wants to stay in
control
and put a few conditions between me
and the one who I am asked to forgive.

(HN, *The Return of the Prodigal Son*)

Silent Reflection

The Canticle of Zachary

> God be blessed!
> I now am free, because I belong to God...

Prayers of Gratitude

The Lord's Prayer

Sharing of the Peace / The Sign of the Cross

> May God bless us, free us from all harm,
> and lead us to life everlasting. Amen.

Monday Evening Prayer

Invitatory / The Sign of the Cross

Optional Song or Hymn

Psalm 136:1–9

> *Where there is charity, where there is love.*
> *God is there.*

God's love is unending!

God is good,
   the God of Gods!
God's love is unending!

God is the creator of all worlds!
God's love is unending!

God is the designer of the skies!
God's love is unending!

God laid out the land on the sea!
God's love is unending!

God turned on the great lights!
God's love is unending!

God welcomed the sun!
God's love is unending!

God brought forth the stars,
   the moon; the darkness!
God's love is unending!

(DH, adapt.)

Pause for Silent Prayer

Psalm 136:10–26

> *All of the deeds of God are awesome and
> wonderful.*

God is our escape from bondage, by the arm of
power!
God's love is unending!

God split the sea in two!
God's love is unending!

God let Israel cross over!
God's love is unending!

God drowned Pharaoh and his armies!
God's love is unending!

God led us through the desert!
God's love is unending!

God neutralized the enemy tribes and conquered
the evil monarchs!
God's love is unending!

God gave Israel a beautiful land!
God's love is unending!

God never forgot our suffering!
God's love is unending!

God always brings a victory!
God's love is unending!

God sustains all living things!
God's love is unending!

God be given thanks in the highest heaven!
God's love is unending!

(DH, adapt.)

From Henri

My daily hour with God
is not a time of deep prayer
in which I contemplate the divine mysteries
or feel a special closeness to God.
On the contrary,
it is full of distractions, inner restlessness,
confusion, and boredom.
It seldom, if ever, pleases my senses.
Even though I do not feel God's love
the way I feel a human embrace,
even though I do not hear a voice
as I hear human words of consolation,
even though I do not see a smile
like I see a human face,
still the Lord speaks to me, looks at me,
and embraces me there.

(HN, *Discernment: Reading the Signs of Daily Life*)

Silent Reflection

The Canticle of Mary

My soul is bursting with how great God is!
My spirit cannot stop rejoicing...

Prayers of Intercession

The Lord's Prayer

Sharing of the Peace / The Sign of the Cross

May God bless us, free us from all harm,
and lead us to life everlasting. Amen.

Tuesday Morning Prayer

Invitatory / The Sign of the Cross

Optional Song or Hymn

Psalm 101:1–3a, 7–8

> *You, O God, are my song.*
> *Let the music sing of your truth.*

My song,
>   my music,
>   is the tonality of justice and love.

All that is alive and all that is true
>   drives my rhythm,
>   and it transforms
>   the central nervous system of my life
>   into an energy
>   that is consumed with you.

So, where are you?
When you will come to me?

I will move step by step
>   with a blameless heart;
I will shun what is false—
>   not allowing it to come near.

I want the loyal to dwell with me—
>   those who live in deceit
>   are not welcome.

Every morning—
    today,
    and tomorrow's tomorrow—
    I ache to purify
    and restore God's glorious city.

(DH, adapt.)

Pause for Silent Prayer

Psalm 144

A new song I will sing to you, O God.

Praise and blessing!
You, my rock!

You, strength for the conflict.
You, my hands for the challenge.
You, my wall of safety.
You, my castle.
You, my deepest love.
You, my victory.

How is it that you always care for us?
How is it that you always give more
    than just the time of day?
We are a mere breath,
    a puff of smoke,
    and our days are like passing shadows.

Bend the sky downward,
    and touch the mountains -
    caress them until they explode into flames!

Strike the lightning and thunderbolts,
  and let the arrows soar!
Pluck me out from the terror of the waters
  and the grip of the strangers
  who seduce by their lies.

A brand new and vibrant song
  I will sing for you—
  I will strum and play my praises,
  for yours is the music of finishing first;
  you rescue David from the sword.

You mold your sons and daughters
  like the plants that grow vigorously
  and the cornerstones that are dug deep.

You feed our barns to the full
  with endless grain;
  the sheep bless our fields,
  and the oxen are numerous and strong.

Protection is mighty.
There is no breaking in or breaking out—
  no shouting in the streets.

Happy are all of us who live like this!
Happy are all of us who give our lives to you,
  fully and without reserve!

We are blest!

(DH, adapt.)

From Henri

The spiritual life can be lived
in as many ways as there are people.
What is new is that we have moved

from the many things
to the kingdom of God.
What is new is that we are set free
from the compulsions of our world
and have set our hearts
on the only necessary thing.

(HN, *Making All Things New: An Invitation to the Spiritual Life*)

Silent Reflection

The Canticle of Zachary

God be blessed!
I now am free, because I belong to God...

Prayers of Gratitude

The Lord's Prayer

Sharing of the Peace / The Sign of the Cross

May God bless us, free us from all harm,
and lead us to life everlasting. Amen.

Tuesday Evening Prayer

Invitatory / The Sign of the Cross

Optional Song or Hymn

Psalm 137:1–6, 8

> *We were weeping at Babylon's waters—*
> *we hung up our harps.*

Weeping, weeping,
  remembering Zion.

The willows were bent low—
  there we hung our harps.

In our exile,
  we were tormented and shamed
  into singing
  "happy songs of Zion."

Sarcasm.
Humiliation.

How could we possibly
  sing such songs
  in such a place,
  so foreign to our well being?

Forget Jerusalem?
Forget God's people?
Never.

Let my hand be paralyzed
        and fall off
        instead of losing my memory!
May my voice be silenced,
        if I forget to turn back toward you,
        and celebrate my joy.

Babylon—be doomed!
May you be covered in cursing
        for what you have done!

You deserve evil for evil.
May good rest upon those
        who have smashed your children
        upon the rocks.

(DH, adapt.)

Pause for Silent Prayer

Psalm 138:1–2, 6–8

> *Joining the choir of heaven,*
> *we praise with all our love.*

I thank you, God,
        with all that I am.

I join the music of heaven
        to praise your name,
        for you have listened to the poor,
        and you increase their strength.

The moment I call out—
 you respond.

No hesitation.

You sit high—
 but you look low,
 always loving.

Whether you are very close
 or far away,
 you always seem to know...
 yes, you always know.

When I am afraid,
 you keep me breathing;
 you keep me alive.

You lift me up with your hand,
 rescue-filled.

My cause becomes your cause.

My need for your love
 is always satisfied.

Stay,
 please stay,
 do not leave what you have created.

Keep listening,

Stay.

(DH, adapt.)

From Henri

> The way I become aware of God's presence
> is in that remarkable desire
> to return to that quiet place
> and be there without any real satisfaction....
> God is greater than my senses,
> greater than my thoughts,
> greater than my heart.
> I do believe that God touches me in places
> that are hidden even to myself.
> And I do believe
> that when I pray I am in touch
> with the divine presence reflected in my heart.

(HN, *Discernment: Reading the Signs of Daily Life*)

Silent Reflection

The Canticle of Mary

> My soul is bursting with how great God is!
> My spirit cannot stop rejoicing...

Prayers of Intercession

The Lord's Prayer

Sharing of the Peace / The Sign of the Cross

> May God bless us, free us from all harm,
> and lead us to life everlasting. Amen.

Wednesday Morning Prayer

Invitatory / The Sign of the Cross

Optional Song or Hymn

Psalm 108:2–7

> *Your love, O God, expands and expands,*
> *reaching beyond the galaxies.*

I have decided,
    for my heart is ready,
    ready to sing and offer praise.
My harp and lyre are prepared
    and so I can—
    and I will—
    wake up the dawn.

My voice is lifted and freed
    to sing about you, God,
    to everyone, everywhere -
    about your endless love,
    mercy,
    and truth.

Even the skies will hear my song!

Rise high above the tip of heaven!
Fill the earth with your boundless glory!
Bring deliverance to all those
    whom you love.
Come now, and deliver us all!

(DH, adapt.)

Pause for Silent Prayer

Psalm 146:1–4, 6b–10

> *With all I am,*
> *with everything I have,*
> *I praise God.*

Every part of me,
    my soul,
    my body,
    every inch of me
    wants to honor and praise God,
    as long as I can,
    as long as I will live.

It is not wise
    to lay your trust
    with mere human leaders—
    they will disappoint!
Once they die,
    their promises decay.
But with God—
    all moves on,
    the future is secure!

It is very wise
    to trust God's vision,
    for God is the maker of everything,
    and always keeps faith with us!

God is food for the starving,
>> justice for the poor and hopeless,
>> freedom for those held captive.

Eyes are opened!
Limbs that are bent
>> are made straight!
Widows and orphans
>> are no longer alone!
Strangers are welcomed:
>> no longer aliens!

God,
>> give out love
>> to those who live justice;
>> and subvert all
>> who deprive
>> anyone of dignity.

Praise God!
God is forever!
So, likewise,
>> our praise is forever!

Life leads to more life!

(DH, adapt.)

From Henri

> God does not require our success,
> popularity, or power in order to love us.
> Once we discern our identity
> and accept God's unconditional love,
> we are free to live in the world
> without being owned by the world.

We can forgive those who hurt or disappoint us
without letting bitterness, jealousy,
or resentment enter our hearts.
The most beautiful fruit of *claiming your
belovedness*
is a joy that allows us to share
God's unconditional love with others.
Strange as it may sound,
we can become like God for others.

(HN, *Discernment: Reading the Signs of Daily Life*)

Silent Reflection

The Canticle of Zachary

God be blessed!
I now am free, because I belong to God...

Prayers of Gratitude

The Lord's Prayer

Sharing of the Peace / The Sign of the Cross

May God bless us, free us from all harm,
and lead us to life everlasting. Amen.

Wednesday Evening Prayer

Invitatory / The Sign of the Cross

Optional Song or Hymn

Psalm 139:1–10

> *God, I am overwhelmed by you.*
>
> You know me.
> Your beam goes right through me:
>> and sees everything,
>> understands everything,
>> finds everything—
>> and knows.
>
> Everything.
>
> When I sit,
>> when I stand,
>> all my thoughts—
>> before they even begin
>> to arrive in my mind—
>> you have knowledge of it all.
>
> Even before I attempt to speak,
>> you know it already
>> and you speak it.
> You are behind, before,
>> with your gentle hand
>> calmly touching me—
>> wherever I am
>> or may be planning to go.

It is impossible for my mind
    and my heart
    to wrap around this mystery.
It is incomprehensible.
I cannot begin to grasp it.

Where could I possibly go to escape you?
How could I even imagine fleeing from you
    and removing myself from your presence?

If I ascend toward heaven—there you are.
If I descend to the bottom of this world—there you are.
Your grip and hold on me
    is everywhere,
    in every way:
    if I fly toward the rising of the morning,
    if I go down to the depths of the sea,
    you are there.

You are there.

(DH, adapt.)

Pause for Silent Prayer

Psalm 139:13–18

Search me, probe me.
Lead me, O God.

Every part of me—
    you created,

and you placed me
in the warm waters
of my mother's womb.
What a wonder this is!
My gratitude is bursting.

You have embroidered me
into your fabric—
I am your material;
your garment in this physical world.

You have noted
and kept record
of my every moment,
long before such moments
could be imagined.

Your thoughts—
so treasured and precious!
Their depth,
beyond anything I could ever know.

You know me so well.
Actually,
you know me too well.

(DH, adapt.)

From Henri

Prayer, contemplation, meditation,
solitude, silence—
they are all meant to develop an awareness
of the voice in your heart that says,
"I loved you
long before you could have loved one another.

I accepted you
long before you could accept one another.
I embraced you
long before you could hold one another."
This is how we will find our freedom.

(HN, *The Return of the Prodigal Son*)

Silent Reflection

The Canticle of Mary

My soul is bursting with how great God is!
My spirit cannot stop rejoicing...

Prayers of Intercession

The Lord's Prayer

Sharing of the Peace / The Sign of the Cross

May God bless us, free us from all harm,
and lead us to life everlasting. Amen.

Thursday Morning Prayer

Invitatory / The Sign of the Cross

Optional Song or Hymn

Psalm 143:8

> *I will proclaim your love in the morning, my God.*
> *I trust you.*

> May I,
>   this morning,
>   be an announcement
>   of your love,
>   for it is in you alone
>   that I place my trust.
> Show me
>   and guide me in ways that are right.

> I offer you myself.
> Everything I have.
> Everything I am.

> (DH, adapt.)

Pause for Silent Prayer

Psalm 147:1–6a

> *It is so good and right to offer God praise!*
> *Make noise!*

> It is so good!
> Sing it!

It is so good
　　to praise,
　　to give thanks
　　to this God of ours
　　who makes no distinctions
　　in pouring out mercy.

God rebuilds us,
　　restores us,
　　gathers
　　and regathers us,
　　over and over again—
　　and never gets tired
　　of lavishing us with mercy.

Broken hearts are healed.
Our wounds are attended to,
　　and wrapped in love.
Every star is given a name—
　　and so are we.
We are so unbelievably
　　known by God,
　　who keeps calling us
　　by the dignity of our names.

God's power is endless;
God's wisdom reaches above
　　and visits us,
　　fills us,
　　and changes us.

When we are bent over,
>   you help us to stand tall—
>   you strengthen and sustain.

(DH, adapt.)

From Henri

So who am I? Who are you?
We are God's beloved ones,
bearers of the divine image
and human beings capable of glory and goodness
as well as harm and alienation.
We need to hear again and again
that we are the beloved of God....
When we understand the mystery
that we are loved not for what we do
but because of who God says we are,
we are free to love others in a similar way.

(HN, *Discernment: Reading the Signs of Daily Life*)

Silent Reflection

The Canticle of Zachary

God be blessed!
I now am free, because I belong to God...

Prayers of Gratitude

The Lord's Prayer

Sharing of the Peace / The Sign of the Cross

May God bless us, free us from all harm,
and lead us to life everlasting. Amen.

Thursday Evening Prayer

Invitatory / The Sign of the Cross

Optional Song or Hymn

Psalm 144:1–8

> *You are my love, my safety, my protection.*
> *You are my God.*
>
> Praise and blessing!
> You, my rock!
>
> You, strength for the conflict.
> You, my hands for the challenge.
> You, my wall of safety.
> You, my castle.
> You, my deepest love.
> You, my victory.
>
> How is it that you always care for us?
> How is it that you always give more
>   than just the time of day?
> We are a mere breath,
>   a puff of smoke,
>   and our days are like passing shadows.
>
> Bend the sky downward,
>   and touch the mountains—
>   caress them until they explode into flames!
> Strike the lightning and thunderbolts,
>   and let the arrows soar!

Pluck me out from the terror of the waters
    and the grip of the strangers
    who seduce by their lies.

(DH, adapt.)

Pause for Silent Prayer

Psalm 144:9–15

You are our joy, and our greatest gift, O God.

A brand new and vibrant song
    I will sing for you—
    I will strum and play my praises,
    for yours is the music of finishing first,
    you rescue David
    from the sword.

You mold your sons and daughters
    like the plants that grow vigorously,
    and the cornerstones that are dug deep.

You feed our barns to the full
    with endless grain;
    the sheep bless our fields,
    and the oxen are numerous and strong.

Protection is mighty
There is no breaking in or breaking out—
    no shouting in the streets.

Happy are all of us who live like this!
Happy are all of us who give our lives to you,
    fully and without reserve!

We are blest!

(DH, adapt.)

From Henri

It might sound strange
to consider grief a way to compassion.
But it is.
Grief asks me to allow the sins of the world—
my own included—
to pierce my heart and make me shed tears,
many tears, for them.
There is no compassion without many tears.
If they can't be tears that stream from my eyes,
they have to be at least tears
that well up from my heart.

(HN, *The Return of the Prodigal Son*)

Silent Reflection

The Canticle of Mary

My soul is bursting with how great God is!
My spirit cannot stop rejoicing....

Prayers of Intercession

The Lord's Prayer

Sharing of the Peace / The Sign of the Cross

May God bless us, free us from all harm,
and lead us to life everlasting. Amen.

Friday Morning Prayer

Invitatory / The Sign of the Cross

Optional Song or Hymn

Psalm 51:12–19

> *Take my heart, O God, and make a change.*
> *Even out my spirit.*

Make clean and clear away
    all of the dust and debris
    from my heart.
Come and bring a steadiness,
    a smooth path to my spirit.
Do not abandon me—
    hold me tightly to your presence.

Help me,
    convince me
    that joy will follow pain.

Sustain and support me;
    and know
    that I will provide the direction
    to those who need
    to return to you.

Stop the tears
    so I will be able to sing a song
    love-packed with the taste of you.

Provide for my voice
    to clearly become a shout
    of praise to you.

Courage.
Bring courage to my heart.

Sacrifices will not work.
They do not satisfy you.
So then,
    I offer you my broken self:
    my fragile heart,
    my tender spirit.

These things you welcome.

You will not turn away,
    because you have my heart.

(DH, adapt.)

Pause for Silent Prayer

Psalm 147:12–16, 19–20

Zion—praise God.
For God is speaking to us—the Word is alive!

Listen well, Jerusalem!
Zion, be attentive and praise!

God has kept you safe,
    for you are locked in and protected,

provided with children,
peaceful in your homes,
and fed well with the finest of wheat.

God continues to speak:
Word proclaimed, spoken, shouted!
Snow sprinkles down like diamonds,
frost sows like the dust
and is scattered about,
chased away by the melting wind.

God speaks the Word;
to all of you, the direction is given.
You alone, O Jacob,
are the landing point and target
for God's voice.

No one else can hear!

(DH, adapt.)

From Henri

You have to celebrate your chosenness constantly.
This means saying "thank you" to God
for having chosen you,
and "thank you" to all
who remind you of your chosenness.
Gratitude is the most fruitful way
of deepening your consciousness
that you are not an "accident,"
but a divine choice.

(HN, *Life of the Beloved*)

Silent Reflection

The Canticle of Zachary

> God be blessed!
> I now am free, because I belong to God...

Prayers of Gratitude

The Lord's Prayer

Sharing of the Peace / The Sign of the Cross

> May God bless us, free us from all harm,
> and lead us to life everlasting. Amen.

Friday Evening Prayer

Invitatory / The Sign of the Cross

Optional Song or Hymn

Psalm 145:2–5, 10–11

> *Each and every day I will bless you*
> *and marvel on your ways.*

Every day,
    every moment,
    every thought,
    every action—
    all give praise!
No end in sight,
    only beginning
    again and again.

Always new.

"Always great" is who
    and what you are—
    what you always do.

Too infinite to capture,
    too amazing,
    too deep.

The stories of praising you
    are passed down
    and down—

singing splendor;
glorious majesty;
works of wonder!

Everything is percolating,
exposing gratitude—
transformed into blessing,
a most faithful blessing,
singing of your city of justice,
and the wisdom of your ways.

(DH, adapt.)

Pause for Silent Prayer

Psalm 145:13c-16, 19–21

Every one and every thing—all look to you, God.
You are near when we call.

Faithful ones, give praise!
Blessings, give praise!
Glory upon glory, give praise!
All things and creatures
give witness—
declare,
proclaim!

God is faithful.
God is gracious.
God is holy.
God is "always there."

Present.

Lifting up fallen ones,
    raising up lowly ones.
God, we all look to you,
    and you feed us when it is time.
Your hands, always open,
    answering and responding,
    filling our desire.

You keep us alive!

May the singing never end;
    may the praising never end;
    may the blessing never end,
    tomorrow and beyond!

Always:
    that means, "forever!"

(DH, adapt.)

From Henri

As I reflect on my life....
I still feel like the least of God's holy people....
I realize that I am still struggling
with the same problems I had all those years ago.
Notwithstanding my many prayers, periods of retreat,
advice from friends, and time with counselors and
confessors,
it seems that very little, if anything, has changed.
I am still the restless, nervous, intense, distracted,
and impulse-driven person I was
when I set out on this spiritual journey.
I am still searching for inner peace and unity

and a resolution to my many internal conflicts....
So, "who will rescue me?"
I pray with Saint Paul.
"Thanks be to God
through Jesus Christ our Lord!"
(Rom. 7:15-25 NRSV).

(HN, *Discernment: Reading the Signs of Daily Life*)

Silent Reflection

The Canticle of Mary

My soul is bursting with how great God is!
My spirit cannot stop rejoicing...

Prayers of Intercession

The Lord's Prayer

Sharing of the Peace / The Sign of the Cross

May God bless us, free us from all harm,
and lead us to life everlasting. Amen.

Saturday Morning Prayer

Invitatory / The Sign of the Cross

Optional Song or Hymn

Psalm 92

> *It is so good to thank you.*

It is so good,
>> even though it is challenging—
>> to give thanks and praise
>> to your unsayable name:

In the morning light
>> we remember
>> your amazing kindness;
>> with the night sky
>> we call to mind and ponder
>> your most faithful heart.

We sing about these things,
>> and so much more,
>> with every instrument
>> we can get our hands on,
>> because every deed of yours
>> demands a song!

Everything you do
>> is stunning;
>> you are at work in everything,
>> and we become animated
>> by your stirrings—
>> too deep to comprehend!

To not be taken in by you
    is to be so utterly foolish.
There are scoundrels out there,
    springing up like weeds.
They begin to bloom,
    but they cannot sustain any growth—
    thus they are mowed down.

But you cannot be mowed down
    because those who oppose you
    become scattered and are cast away.

You strengthen us,
    and anoint us with new resolve:
    we glisten and grow;
    brighten and glow;
    and are given fresh eyes
    so we can see clearly;
    fresh ears
    so we can hear
    and tune out
    the noise of those who bring harm.

So we will grow justly
    like palm trees!
We will rise up majestically
    like the cedars of Lebanon!
We will be planted in your house,
    and our leaves eternally green,
    rustling in your courtyard.

Even though we will grow old,
    our branches will flourish,
    stay vigorous,
    covered with foliage.

We will remain your emblem of justice.
We will be sealed
    with no possible cracks to be found.

(DH, adapt.)

Pause for Silent Prayer

Psalm 8

*Even the incomprehensible cries of children
sing, declare, and praise you, O God.*

It is impossible
    to pin you down,
    to contain you,
    to name you adequately.

Your name is too beautiful
    and filled with glory—
    it moves and dances
    beyond my sight,
    beyond my mind,
    landing and stirring in my heart.

Your presence—
    extends beyond imagination
    to imagination,
    mystery bound,
    always outward,
    further and further
    beyond my senses,
    beyond the planets and stars.

Even the mouths of the newborn
        make their wordless sounds to you:
        strength too impossible to fathom;
        power too mighty to ponder;
        enemies brought down.

I behold the night sky
        and the work of your hands:
        the bright moon
        and the sparkling stars
        that you made.

And then I think:

Who is woman,
        so frail—
        that you remember her?
Who is man,
        so small—
        that you keep him in mind?
Who are any of us,
        so insignificant—
        that you care at all?

But beyond all reason,
        you hold us all as angels,
        as gods,
        as holy!

You have crowned us
        in your own splendor.
You have empowered us
        to take charge,
        to take care of your creation:

Sheep and cattle,
        flocks of birds

and herds of deer,
the goats and the cows,
and the fish
who dart about in the sea.

Your name is too beautiful
and filled with glory!

(DH, adapt.)

From Henri

Each of us has a mission in life.
"What does God want from me?"
is a question we all ask,
not once and for all but throughout our lives.
New vocations are full of promise.
Something very important is in store for us.
There is a hidden treasure to discover.
But I learned that my deeper vocation
is to announce God's love for all people.
My final destination is not a place;
it is God's eternal embrace.

(HN, *Discernment: Reading the Signs of Daily Life*; DH, adapt.)

Silent Reflection

The Canticle of Zachary

God be blessed!
I now am free, because I belong to God...

Prayers of Gratitude

The Lord's Prayer

Sharing of the Peace / The Sign of the Cross

May God bless us, free us from all harm,
and lead us to life everlasting. Amen.

Psalm-Poems for Midday Prayer

When we remain faithful to our discipline,
even if it is only ten minutes a day,
we gradually come to see—
by the candlelight of our prayers -
that there is a space within us where God dwells
and where we are invited to dwell with God.
Once we come to know that inner, holy place,
a place more beautiful and precious
than any place we can travel to,
we want to be there and spiritually fed.

(HN, *Here and Now: Living in the Spirit*)

The Psalm-Poems that you find here are adapted from the suggested psalms ascribed for Midday Prayer.

The structure of Midday Prayer is very simple:

- The singing of an optional song or hymn
- The praying of one or more psalms (chosen from those provided on pp. 215–222)
- A short reading or, in keeping with the lens of the morning and evening prayer settings in this resource, a reflection from the words of Henri Nouwen
- A closing prayer

This is only a suggested structure that is in keeping with the traditional ritual form of Midday Prayer. Individuals and groups should feel free to be creative and adapt the structure according to the needs of the setting and occasion.

Psalm-Poems for Midday Prayer

Psalm 23

> If God is my shepherd—
>> and indeed that is so—
>> there is nothing at all that I will need.
> The field of green is my resting place,
>> near a well of water;
>> my spirit is now alive again—and full.
>
> You guide me,
>> true to your name.
> If I make my way through
>> the darkest turns,
>> I know you are with me.
>
> You bring a shepherd's care.
>
> The table is laid out before me,
>> full and glorious,
>> as hate gathers close.
> Oil anoints and travels
>> deep into the pores of my skin,
>> bringing healing;
>> cups filled, brimming.
>
> Love will follow;
>> goodness will accompany me
>> throughout my life.
> I will be brought to God's door,
>> and I will find my home—
>> my final reach.
>> Forever.

(DH, adapt.)

Psalm 25

My soul is given freely
and totally—
to you.

I open wide
the trust that occupies my heart.
Please,
do not close its door.

Teach me how to live.
Show me, God, your way.
Direct and point me to your truth:
you, my God who saves;
you, my God,
my endless hope.

Do not forget your tender mercy,
your endless love.

Remember the best of me,
not my flaws,
the choices of my youth.

Goodness.
Show goodness.
Remember the very best in me.

My soul.
Reaching out and up.
Meet me there.

Bring clarity to my life;
guide me.
Truth-teller, teacher,
savior.
I am waiting.

Reveal your goodness;
    I am holding on for direction.

Humble me.
Bring justice.
Humble me more.
Your way then becomes clear.

To be tethered to you
    on your road
    is a path of blessed kindness,
    consistency,
    covenant.
I honor you
    and seek your holy friendship.
Your promise is my map.

(DH, adapt.)

Psalm 34:2–3, 16–17, 18–19

Every day, every hour,
    every moment
I will show gratitude,
    blessing, and thanks.

With every word I sing,
    I sing of God's richness,
    God's goodness—
    everyone listen:
    may our souls glisten
    and glory together;
    may the lowly ones hear,
    and be filled with rejoicing!

God's eyes look out for the just,
    and his ears listen to their cries.

God knows and confronts those
    who choose evil
    and brings an end to their ways.

Cry out, you just ones—God is listening!
Cry out, you who are in distress—God rescues!

God is so very near indeed,
    to our broken hearts.
God cries with us
    when our spirits are crushed.

And God saves us.

(DH, adapt.)

Psalm 71:1–6

I really do believe in You.
I look to You,
    now,
    desperately—
    do not allow me to look foolish.

I need You.
    I am in need of a freedom
    that only You can give –
I am in need of rescue,
    for I feel danger coming near.

I need the strength
    that comes only from You:
    You, my fortress:
    strong, firm, invincible.

Help.
Please.

Set me free
> from the stranglehold
> that has me by the throat.

Feeling trapped.

You are the only hope I have.
It has been so
> ever since I was young.
Since my mother's womb,
> You have been the one
> whom I have leaned on,
> over and over again.

I am now,
> leaning again,
> on You.

I cannot find the words
> to thank You,
> to praise You.

(DH, adapt.)

Psalm 102:26–28

> From ages past
> > you made, built,
> > and crafted this earth.
> The sky and the heavens—
> > they too—
> > are among
> > your many tremendous compositions.

> But even if they fade,
> > you never will.
> You only become more present.

While our clothing
    becomes old and tattered
    and eventually thrown away,
    you will never wear out;
    never grow thin.

You remain.
There is no "final time" for you.

(DH, adapt.)

Psalm 104:24–30

Amazing!
You have created so much—
    you have created it all!
The earth is bursting
    with all of your creatures—
    with all of the ferment and movement
    that is stirring and buzzing about.

The sea is wide and vast,
    and the creatures it holds
    are too many to number—
    all things that live and breathe,
    small and great.

Everything looks,
    and points to you
    for nurture
    when the time is right.
You offer it,
    and they all pull it together
    and gather it up.
Your hands are wide open—
    filling everything.

When you hide your presence,
       they are sad.
    If you take away their very breath,
       they die—
       and return to their dusty beginnings.
    But when your spirit blows and turns
       and enters their spirit—
       all is made new!

The earth is renewed!

(DH, adapt.)

Psalm 128

We are full of happiness and bliss;
    in awe,
    standing in your presence.
How rich is your table,
    the bounty of your hands!
Your beloved one
    is like the vine bearing rich fruit,
    warm from your presence.

Children circle 'round this table,
    like olive saplings—
    such a blessing they are!
Blessings abound
    when we honor God.

May we know God's blessing
    and receive the gift
    of such precious happiness.
May Jerusalem,
    and may all of us,
    live to see our grandchildren.

And one day—

    in our journey of questions and struggle,
    may we know the peace
    that comes from God above.

(DH, adapt.)

Psalm-Poems for Night Prayer

Much of Jesus' prayer took place during the night.
"Night" means more than the absence of the sun.
It also means the absence of satisfying feelings
or enlightening insights.
That's why it is so hard to be faithful.
But God is greater than our hearts and minds
and keeps calling us the beloved—
far beyond all feelings and thoughts.

(HN, *Here and Now: Living in the Spirit*)

The Psalm-Poems that you find here are adapted from the suggested psalms ascribed for Night Prayer (or Compline)—the time of prayer just before going to sleep.

The structure of Night Prayer is very simple:

- A brief beginning asking for God's forgiveness
- An optional song or hymn; or the reading of an antiphon provided below
- The praying of one or more psalms (chosen from those provided on pg. 226–233)
- A short reading or, in keeping with the lens of the morning and evening prayer settings in this resource, a reflection from the words of Henri Nouwen
- The Canticle of Simeon (which is included here)
- A closing prayer and blessing
- The singing of a hymn to Mary, the Mother of God (in the customary Night Prayer tradition)

This is only a suggested structure that is in keeping with the traditional ritual form of Night Prayer. Individuals and groups should feel free to be creative and adapt the structure according to the needs of the setting and occasion.

Antiphon for Night Prayer

Protect us God, as we are still awake;
keep watch over us in our sleeping,
so that while we are awake
we may be attentive with Christ,
and while we are asleep, rest in his peace.

(St. Augustine, DH, adapt.)

Psalm-Poems for Night Prayer

Psalm 4:1–2, 4–9

God, answer me when I call to you.
You are the one
    who released me from my troubles—
    so please,
    continue to be good to me.
Listen to my prayer.

Look! Listen!
God confounds all who believe.
God listens when I call.

Tremble, but do not be afraid.
Be attentive to your heart,
    and be peaceful throughout the night.

Pray with integrity.
Trust in God.

Those who doubt, they say,
    "Who will bless us?
    Even this God has abandoned us."

But you, O God,
    fill my heart with more joy
    than all of the grain and wine
    that the cynics provide.

I will sleep secure this night.
You continue to care for me.

(DH, adapt.)

Psalm 31:10–16a

Be gracious, God,
> for I feel a deep and painful ache
> all over.
My eyes are tired and beaten;
> my heart is exhausted;
> I am filled with great dissatisfaction.

My sighs are just too deep,
> so much so
> that nothing else can get through.
My strength is completely tapped.
My bones are rickety.

I am insulted
> over and over—
I am avoided,
> forgotten,
> like the dead.
I am like a horror to my friends.

But yet,
> I still choose to trust you.
> I still believe
> without reserve or hesitation
> that you hold my life
> in your hands.

(DH, adapt.)

Psalm 88:2–3, 10b–11, 14–15, 17–19

I now know
> that you are my life,
> and my only help.

From the distance at day,
   I cry out to you.
At night—
   I am here,
   vulnerable,
   waiting for you to come to me.

May my prayer touch you—
   and open your ears
   to hear me.

I keep reaching out to you
   all day long—
   my hands are outstretched
   wondering where you are.

Do you not work wonders?
Do you not bring light to the shadows?

My eyes are burning;
   my heart is straining to find you.
Every morning
   I wake up
   and keep offering
   this unending prayer to you.

Why are you throwing me aside?
Why are you hiding?

You anger is like a fire
   sizzling throughout my body.
I am devastated
   by the trials you put me through.

My anxiety is swirling everywhere.
I am drowning.
Pulled down to the bottom.

Feeling closed in.

Can't breathe.

You have stolen my companions from me.
The light has been taken away.

(DH, adapt.)

Psalm 91:1–7, 10:16

All of us who know God's shelter
and rest in God's shadow,
sing to God in hope:

"You are my trust."

God will pull away
all people and things
that hunt you down,
that hold you imprisoned.
You will be covered
with wings that will keep you safe.

You will not be haunted by the night.
You will not be the target of arrows.
You will find your steps at nighttime.
You will not suffer harm at noon.

In the midst of the killing of thousands,
you shall live free,
unscathed;
kept innocent by God's protection.

God will shut out
everything that may cripple your life.

No more harm will come to you.
Angels are keeping watch.

Your feet shall pass over stumbling stones,
    for these are strong angels
      who are always protecting you.

God announces:

"Whoever holds on to me,
    I will set free.
Whoever knows me
    and calls me by name,
    I will answer them,
    and stand by them,
    no matter what,
    in the best
    and in the most frightening of times.

I will always be their rescue.
I will give them life to the full—
    I will have their backs;
    I will be their safety."

(DH, adapt.)

Psalm 103

Mercy!
Bless God, O my soul!
And all that is possible within me,
    bless God's most holy and blessed name.

Mercy!
Remember always, the blessings of God—
    the one who forgives your shortcomings,

the one who heals your afflictions,
>the one who redeems your life from the pit,
>the one who crowns you with unending love
>and compassion,
>the one who satisfies you with only good things,
>the one who does so forever,
>the one who soars within you like an eagle,
>the one who restores your youth.

Mercy!
This God is a God who brings forth justice
>for those who are oppressed.

Merciful.
Gracious,
Slow to anger.
Abounding, bursting forth with love.

Mercy!
This God will not pile on shame and guilt.
Anger lasts barely a moment.
This God does not deal with us according to our
failures.
This God has not, does not, and will not
>haunt us with our sins.

Mercy!
>As high as the heavens are,
>that is the height of God's love
>for all who return to God their honor.
From the rising sun in the east,
>to the setting sun in the west—
>this is the length and breadth of the restoration
>that God provides.

Mercy!
As loving parents have compassion for their
children,
    so does this God, have compassion for us.
God knows us, better than we know ourselves.
God remembers how human we all are.
For the human soul—our days are like the grass—
    flourishing like the beauty of the fields.
    The wind passes over it, and suddenly it is gone.

Mercy!
God's love—now, God's love
    is from everlasting to everlasting
    for the faithful ones,
    those who keep God's covenant,
    and who cherish God's commands.

Mercy!
God sits high,
    but looks and loves— low.

Angels—bless God!
Those with power—bless God!
All who minister to the light—bless God!
All wonders and works—bless God!
Everyone in all places—bless God!

Bless God, O my soul.

Mercy!

(DH, adapt.)

Psalm 134

Bless God,
    and all who serve in God's house.

Bless all
  who keep watch throughout the night.

Lift up your hands in the holy place,
  and bless God.

And may God,
  who designs the entirety of the earth
  and the infinite vastness of the sky,
  bless you, always,
  from Zion.

(DH, adapt.)

Canticle for Night Prayer

Luke 2:29-32

The Canticle of Simeon (Nunc Dimittis)

> God, I am your servant.
> If I must die,
>> I can now make the journey
>> with complete surrender
>> on the wind of your peace,
>> as you promised.
>
> With my eyes—full of heart—
>> I have seen,
>> and see even more clearly now
>> the place of safety
>> that you have made ready
>> for all whom you hold close to your heart.
>
> Revealing light.
> Blazing glory.
> A place among your people.
> I belong to you.

(DH, adapt.)

(*Welcome, Faithful Presence*)

Invitatories, Antiphons, & Canticles

Invitatories

Psalm 95

The Venite

> So here we are:
>> singing to you—
>> infused with passion,
>> leading and erupting, becoming a shout:
>
> Here!
> Now!
> At the place and space
>> where you are present!
>
> We are totally taken
>> with and by you,
>> possessed by you,
>> belonging to you.
>
> So here we are:
>> We celebrate You—
>> because you are the gift of power,
>> a power that no one
>> and no thing
>> can match.
> You have the hands
>> that touch the depths of the earth.
> You are the heart
>> that pierces the mountain's height.
>
> You are the presence
>> that constantly changes the sea

because it is yours—
it belongs to you.

So here we are:
    in awe,
    bringing the earth and the sea
    of our very selves
    to you, here,
    now.

You are the beyond that we follow.
We are the doing—
    the sheep who graze
    close to you,
    inviting you to come
    and shape us,
    and change us.

So here we are:
    listening to your voice,
    hoping to be awakened
    and shaken by your Word:

"Do not lose heart
    as you have before,
    when you became confused
    with the afflictions
    that surrounded you;
    in the days when your parents
    all but lost their faith

as they demanded outward signs
of everything that already is:
my presence.

For forty years
I became and remained bitter,
because they became
a lost people,
blind to my destiny for them.
I then made a vow,
in anger,
that they would never again
enter my house."

So here we are:
in light of all of this.

Here we are.

(DH, adapt.)

Additional Invitatories (DH, adapt.)

ORDINARY TIME
Welcome, faithful presence.

Come and fill my day with new breath,
that I may be a living hymn of praise to you.

As I begin this day,
I thank you that last night
was not my last night.

ADVENT
Maranatha.
Come, Lord Jesus, come.

CHRISTMAS
Welcome, Emmanuel.
God with us.

LENT
May we return to the Lord, our God.

EASTER
Christ is risen, Alleluia!

Morning Prayer

ANTIPHONS

(DH, adapt.)

ORDINARY TIME

Praise God—Israel's God!

God's mercy dawns from the highest place,
shining through, shattering the dark,
loosening the horror and fear of death.

God, light our way to a deep and lasting peace.

ADVENT

Be strong and full of courage!
God's liberation is near.

CHRISTMAS

Give to God the highest glory,
and everlasting peace to all people on earth,
Alleluia.

LENT

To be my disciples,
deny yourselves, take up your cross, and follow me.

EASTER

Give God everlasting thanksgiving
who has provided victory through Christ, Alleluia.

GOSPEL CANTICLE

The Benedictus

God be blessed!
I am now free, because I belong to God.
God is coming, over and over again,
    to raise me up, to open my eyes,
    to dwell in my heart, to rescue my life.

The voices of friends and messengers
    have entered into my space,
    they are sent every day,
    sharing and announcing to me the amazing truth
    that all that is evil, in the end, will not win;
    that hate cannot and will not poison and infect
    the wonderful and good that is in me—
    in all of us.

Mercy abounds!
Promises kept!
Covenant sealed!

I once was imprisoned by darkness,
    and I am now filled with light.
I was once paralyzed and unable to praise,
    now my doors of joy fling open without fear.
I, all of us, are holy, beloved;
    vessels of justice in God's eyes.
    Always.

I am the beloved;
    I am an ambassador,
    a witness to this most holy presence.
I must announce, prepare,
    and have my eyes, ears and heart be opened
    to continually and humbly receive the story

of how God is loving,
of how God is saving,
of how God forgives all of us,
over and over again.

Tenderness.
Compassion.
These are my names for God,
who dawns from the highest place,
shining through,
shattering the dark,
protecting me in my deepest corners,
loosening the stranglehold of hate,
and the horror and fear of death.

For God decides,
and will always choose
to guide my way,
and forever lead me
to a deep and lasting peace.

Luke 1:68-79 (DH, adapt.)

(*Welcome, Faithful Presence*)

MORE CANTICLES FOR MORNING PRAYER

Exodus 15:1-18

The Canticle of Moses and Miriam

God is my strength; praise is my song.

God,
God alone is my song!
And this song,
    is filled and fused together
    with triumph!
God has taken the enemy
    and empowered the earth and sea
    to consume them all!

God is strength!
God is "saving-presence!"
This is the song I offer to God,
    the God who comes before all others.

God is true to this name!
God leads us with strength
    hurling over the side,
    into the waters,
    all who strike out against us!

The most feared warriors
    sink quickly into the sea;
    like heavy rocks
    they fall to the bottoms of the deep.

God, you are power beyond power.
You bring evil to its knees,
    you protect us from our foes,
    you set ablaze all that is unjust!

You confound all strategies
    that seek to move against you.

No one can conquer you!
No one can even attempt
    to match your holiness!

What a story this is!
What wonder fills this tale!
    For you stretched out your hand,
    and the earth swallowed them all!

And at the same time—
    the love that you hold in your heart
    redeems and saves,
    clearing a path to your holy place.

When nations and peoples
    seek to rise up against you,
    they shake with fear,
    trembling and shuddering.
When they come to know
    who you are,
    they retreat and melt away.

Those who seek evil—
    they fall away silently,
    while we, your people,
    cross over into freedom!

You bring and plant us
    along the grass of the mountain
    that you have chosen for your people.

This is where you make your dwelling!
This is the temple made by your hand!

You, are God!
It is you that we follow!
Forever!

(DH, adapt.)

1 Samuel:2-10

The Canticle of Hannah

I am a song of acclamation to God,
the one who casts down the mighty ones,
and lifts up the poor.

Acclaim and praise this God—
> this God who lifts up the poor,
> this God who shuts down the wicked,
> this God who brings down the rich and selfish.

This God
> comes and reverses all of our expectations.

This God
> walks with us, all of us who remain faithful.

We shout out to God with our loudest voice:
> "You came to our rescue.

You are the only holy one,
> for there is none like you,
> nowhere, anywhere!"

God can see
> when our actions are in line with our words.

God knows
> when we make arrogant claims,
> claims that are totally impossible for us to hold.

With God
> all weaponry is destroyed, all the weak grow
> strong,

those fat and overfed now struggle,
and the frail and the gaunt are filled
and made healthy again.

Those who were once sterile,
    now are abundant with children,
    and those who have borne many, have been halted.

God commands and decides life and death.
God disperses wealth and want.
God holds the key to casting down and lifting up.
God raises the poor from the ghetto,
    and the vulnerable from the smell of poverty,
    so that all may sit high,
    and take their places of dignity.

God is the owner and arbiter of all creation,
    of the entire universe,
    setting the earth on its course.
While God silences the noise of wickedness,
    we walk by God's side.

All who seek harm for us—
    they will be broken.
Heaven is our strength.
God, and only God,
    can be called upon to judge,
    give authority to rulers on the earth,
    and bring success to those anointed for service.

(DH, adapt.)

1 Chronicles 29:10-13

The Canticle of David

> *Awesome and glorious is your name, O God.*

You, and only you,
   are the source of blessing!

Far too many, beyond number,
   are the attributes of your glory:
   power and greatness,
   splendor and honor,
   and on and on and on!

The entire universe—
   the heavens, the earth,
   the stars, and the sun and moon:
   they are yours.

No one comes close to you,
   and we stand in awe of you,
   watching goodness and bounty
   flow from you.

You command everything—
   your hand is strong,
   and your hand makes us strong.

All we can offer is our thanks!
We praise you!

(DH, adapt.)

Judith 16:2-3a, 13-15

The Canticle of Judith

> *Glory is yours!*
> *All powers is yours!*
>
> Take up the tambourine,
>   and let the cymbals crash!
> Let the music rise,
>   rise and dance to God's name!
>
> My song is new:
>
> "All that is good, all that is glorious is yours, O God!
> Yours is a new and fresh power,
>   and we are all amazed!
>
> All creation leans and bends according to your will,
>   for when you speak, everything begins to form;
>   when you breathe, we all breathe and come alive.
> No one can push back—your voice commands us all.
>
> The mountains and seas move to their center.
> The stones soften into mush when you are present,
>   while those of us who honor you are spared."

(DH, adapt.)

Sirach 14:20; 15:3-5a, 6b

> *You are wisdom and insight, O God.*
>
> Knowledge.
> Insight.
> Understanding.
>
> Wisdom is the feast
>   that is the source of our joy.

Wisdom refreshes, nourishes,
    the bread of knowledge,
    the drink of clarity.

We will not stumble
    when we lean on her insight;
    trust flourishes,
    dignity restored.

She will keep all things even,
    not raising us up over another,
    so that all names will last, survive,
    and endure forever.

(DH, adapt.)

Sirach 39:13-16a

Let our praise rise to you
like the sweet fragrance of roses.

God's fragrance is like a rose,
    blooming for God's children
    alongside the flowing waters.

God's fragrance is to be our fragrance,
    like a sweet perfume
    that sings its hymn of praise,
    that celebrates the great things of God.

So we take up this song
    that brings melody and rhythm
    to the name of God.

Sing the song, loudly with thanks:

"Everything that God does and is—is good!"

(DH, adapt.)

Isaiah 2:2-5

Let us climb God's holy mountain
to the house of Jacob's God.

All nations shall move to the summit of the
mountain,
>as the days draw to an end.

Those from alien lands will gather, saying:

"Let us go now and climb this mountain,
>and approach the house of the God of Jacob—
>for this God will guide us
>on the path that we must take."

Zion is the place where teaching sings.
Jerusalem is the home of God's word.

God will bring an end to conflict.
God will reconcile the people.

And then,
>God's people will beat their swords into plows,
>and their spears into pruning hooks.

This will bring about the end to violence,
>where wars will finally end,
>when the desire for killing and destruction
>will be banished forever.

Let us walk in this light:
>the light of God!

(DH, adapt.)

> *Great light in darkness!*
> *Great joy!*

Light comes to the darkness,
    brightening the way for the lost and stumbling.
The land once dimly covered,
    now shines with the radiance of joy!

We are awestruck by the beauty that we see!
Our gladness cannot be contained!
We all celebrate you and only you,
    like the field workers after the completion of
    harvest,
    like soldiers laying their claims to what is left.

Every garment and all props of war
    will be shredded and burned.

Why?

Because a son is now born and here right now—
    among us,
    a blessed gift from God,
    cloaked with power,
    smothered with titles worthy of our singing:

"Wise One,
    Mighty Counselor,
    Hero for All,
    Holy One Forever,
    Prince of Peace!"

This is the one who will rule.
This is the one who will lead
    with a new and different kind of power,

         expanding and bursting
         until peace is secured and lasting—
         and just throughout all time.

All of this will happen,
    because it is what God wants.

(DH, adapt.)

Isaiah 12:1-6

    Praise God!
    Never stop your praise
    of God's blessed name!

I am full of praise for you, O God,
    because you have reversed your anger
    and I bask in your comfort and consolation.

God is my safety,
    and I am no longer afraid;
God is my strength,
    yes—God makes me strong!

You will drink deeply
    from the deep and generous well of God;
leading you to rise up in song:
    "Praise God!
    God's name I proclaim!"

Don't hold back—
    tell everyone you can
    what God does
    and is still doing,
    announce this to all—
    spread this wonderful news!

Keep the singing, constant and strong,
   all of you children of God—
   because in your midst
   is the great and holy one!

(DH, adapt.)

Isaiah 26:1-5, 7-9, 12

Throughout the night, I ache for you.

We give our honor to the name of God;
   we trust, seek, and yearn to be in this presence.

This is our city—
   the result of God's working hands.
Keep the doors open
   so the world can see
   that we are a just people,
   a faithful people.

God guards with peace,
   keeping hearts focused and rested,
   fixed on God,
   trusting in God.

When we give action to our faith, God,
   you keep the path smooth and straight.

This is the road that we take,
   for we move forward in faith,
   seeking you out,
   hoping to find you,
   to honor you.

We long for you all night long
   with the entirety of everything we are.
You teach and lead us in justice,

and the peace that we know
comes from you alone.
All the good that we do,
begins and ends with you.

(DH, adapt.)

Jeremiah 14:17-21

Do not abandon us, O God.

Endless tears.
All day and all night.
All whom I love
have been struck down.

The dead and the dying
seem to be everywhere.
Everyone is in a daze,
not knowing where to go,
not knowing what to do.

Why do you hold us in such contempt?
Why do you reject us?
Why do the wounds keep infecting,
deeper and deeper?

We are desperate for peace.
We are all but hopeless,
in our call for healing.

Terror seems to be winning.

We know we failed, O God;
we are fully aware of our complicity.
We all share in the shame.

We are still holding on,
　　calling out your name,
　　still hoping in you.

Do not leave us alone.
Remember your promises.
Do not go back on your word.

Not now.

(DH, adapt.)

Jeremiah 17:7-8

Never stop trusting
in the only one we can trust—God alone.

We trust in our God.

We know that God is the only sure thing,
　　the only certainty,
　　in whom we can place our hearts and hopes.

We are to be like the trees that stand near the stream,
　　freeing their roots into the water.

They do not fear the burning heat,
　　because their leaves continue to glow,
　　always green.

Even when all seems dry,
　　they remain serene, full of faith,
　　for the fruit still grows.

(DH, adapt.)

Lamentations 5:1-7, 15-17, 19-21

Always remember our suffering, O God.

God,
>	do not forget us,
>	remember our suffering,
>	walk with us in our shame.
We have been robbed,
>	and strangers now inhabit our homes.

We are orphaned—our fathers are gone;
>	our mothers are widowed.
We are poor,
>	and without the life of water,
>	without the warmth of fire,
>	worn out and never able to rest.

Remember,
>	we have been begging for a long time,
>	crying for bread,
>	and with many dying in shame,
>	leaving us to carry their despair.

We have forgotten what joy is,
>	and we do not dance any more.
We are burdened by our sin,
>	and so our hearts are sickened
>	and tears are our constant companion.

We believe, that you, O God,
>	are the God of our lives,
>	the constant source of all that reigns.
So why have you abandoned us
>	and left us for dead?

Come!
>
> Bring us back—
> so our joy may return.

Give us days like we remember:
> days of your generous good.

(DH, adapt.)

Ezekiel 36:24-28

I will always create a new heart in you,
and breathe into you a new spirit.

I will pull you out
> and set you apart from the nations,
> rescue you from exile,
> and lead you home.

You will be refreshed in clean water,
> made clean from all stains—
> made clean as though for the first time.

You will come to receive and embrace
> a new heart,
> and a new spirit.
The hardness that scars your heart
> will be removed,
> and it will be replaced and renewed
> with a heart centered in the flesh.

My spirit will become your spirit,
> and it will lead you toward me,
> and strengthen your faithfulness
> to my desire.

You will live in the land
> that your parents and ancestors were given.

You will be my people.
I will be your God.

(DH, adapt.)

Daniel 3:56-88

The Canticle of Shadrach, Meschach and Abednego

Everyone, everywhere,
bless and praise God!

Everyone bless and praise God!

Beyond the stars,
    on the earth and in the heavens;
    all holy angels,
    all who reside in heaven:

Everyone bless and praise God!

The waters, deep and wide,
    all infused with spirit,
    the sun, the moon,
    the sparkling of heaven:

Everyone bless and praise God!

The storming rains,
    the whirling winds and gales,
    all fire, all that is hot,
    all that is frosted and chilled:

Everyone bless and praise God!

The dew and the snow,
    the ice and all that is frozen,

the sleet and hale,
the nighttime and the day:

Everyone bless and praise God!

All dark and light,
the thunder and the clouds,
the oceans and all lands,
the hills and mountains:

Everyone bless and praise God!

All plants, trees and flowers,
the fountains, ponds, and streams,
the springs, rivers, and seas,
all fish, whales, and all that swim:

Everyone bless and praise God!

All birds and creatures that fly,
all animals and beasts in this world,
all children of this world,
Israel and all nations:

Everyone bless and praise God!

All who minister and serve,
all of the just and faithful ones,
all holy and righteous,
all who have humble hearts:

Everyone bless and praise God!

All creation that is unseen,
all that covers us beyond our sight,

all the cosmos,
everyone, everything:

Everyone bless and praise God!

(DH, adapt.)

Daniel 12:2-3

If we rise, we will shine.

All of us
who sleep in the dry dust of the earth
shall be awakened—
some of us will see the light of unending light,
others will remain frozen in shame
and in a darkness that knows no end.

If we are wise—
we will shine,
brighter than the sky itself.

If we lead and serve with justice,
we will be like the stars
that will never, ever, disappear.

(DH, adapt.)

Hosea 6:1-3, 6

God delights in the love of the faithful ones.

Let us decide, now,
to return to God,
who yes, struck us down,
but now comes to heal us
and mend our wounds;

who revives,
who restores,
who raises us up
to live in God's holy presence.

Let us decide, now,
to know this God,
whose coming to us is sure as the sunrise,
whose mercy and grace
descends upon us like the rain—
holy water to renew the earth.

Let us decide, now,
to delight—
not in sacrifices,
but in the faithful love
and knowledge of God.

(DH, adapt.)

Micah 4:5-7

We choose to walk in the name
of the one God.

Although all people on this earth
walk and move,
following in the name of their own "god,"
we celebrate
and choose
to walk in the name of the one God—
"Our God"—
always.

Listen now to God's announcement:
"On that day that I will choose,

I will gather together
all those who stumble and cannot move,
all those who are on the outside,
all those who are pained and afflicted—
and they,
they will become a remnant in my name,
a nation,
a people— strong!."

(DH, adapt.)

Evening Prayer

ANTIPHONS

(DH, adapt.)

ORDINARY TIME

O Brilliant light,
you are the raging sun of God Most Holy,
the enteral face of God.
Your image is the image of light,
that splashes upon your heavenly home.

O Child born
of the great source of life;
from beginning to end we praise you.
Our voices are lifted high
as we sing the song of your holy name.

O Redeemer of all creation,
as we see the day beginning to leave us,
and as your light continues to shine,
we praise Abba with you,
and we walk in the Spirit,
one in your presence.

(DH, *With Every Note I Sing* / Inspired from the Phos Hilaron)

My soul is bursting of how great God is;
I rejoice in the liberating power of God.

God shakes the false towers to their foundations,
and lifts the lowly to a more glorious place.

God's strength is my hope.

ADVENT

> God, come to us,
> come with peace to free your people.

CHRISTMAS

> Dance and delight in God;
> let your hearts be filled with joy,
> for liberation and freedom has come. Alleluia.

LENT

> Drink deeply from the well of God's mercy,
> and never thirst again.

EASTER

> God, remain with us,
> for the darkness is near
> and the daylight soon will disappear. Alleluia.

GOSPEL CANTICLE

Luke 1:46-55

Magnificat

> My soul is bursting with how great God is!
> My spirit cannot stop rejoicing,
>> and I cannot begin to hold and take in
>> the liberating power of God.

> Why?

> Because God's favor rests on me,
>> in and out of, and because of my brokenness,
>> in my feeble attempts to serve.

> Beginning today,

right here and right now,
and with every day that will follow,
and because God alone determines who I am,
God's name for me: "the beloved"
will keep ringing in my heart.

Relentless.

God has done, and continues to do,
    amazing and spectacular things for me.
Holy things.
    "Holy is God" will be my constant song.

For all who revere and honor God,
    mercy is, and will be, given lavishly.
God's strength is beyond any hope I have,
    freeing me from the tyranny of self.

If I sit too high—
    if I put too much faith in my own power,
    God will shake my false towers to their
    foundation.

If I find myself drowning in quicksand,
    I will be lifted up to a higher,
    and a more glorious, place.

When I hunger and ache,
    I will be filled and healed.
When I am too comfortable and secure,
    in and through things that are shallow,
    my comfort will become afflicted.
Then, redirected.
Restored.

When I am faithful, I am protected.
Mercy is lavishly given,
      promises are honored and kept.

I am God's beloved child.
I will never be forgotten.

(DH, adapt.)

(*Welcome, Faithful Presence*)

Ephesians 1:3-10

> *In the perfection of time,*
> *God chose to adopt us in Christ.*

Bless our God!
Blessed be the one
>> who is both Father and Mother—
>> the source of the Christ,
>> who blessed us from heaven
>> through the presence of this Christ
>> and the lavish blessings of the spirit.

Before there was anything else,
>> God chose us,
>> infused with this Christ—
>> the living, divine, AND human face of God—
>> to live, breathe, and nurture holiness.

We belong to God!
We are adopted daughters and sons
>> through Christ
>> to be the praise-filled
>> and glory-consumed grace
>> gifted to us all,
>> in the most beloved of all.

The outpouring of Christ
>> is our source of hope and promise,
>> for our brokenness is showered with mercy
>> through a love beyond our imagination.

God, in total freedom,
>> and packed with wisdom and light,

> has revealed to us all
> what was always meant to be:

A timeless road of completeness
> to pull us together:

All of creation,
> marvelously made
> in and through Christ.

(DH, adapt.)

Philippians 2:5-11

> *Jesus humbled himself and embraced the cross.*
> *Jesus Christ is Lord!*

Let your mind and your thoughts and attitudes
> take in and become
> the same mind of Christ Jesus.

For although he was present here,
> with us,
> in the form of God—
> this Jesus,
> this Christ,
> never sought
> and never began
> to think
> or choose to see his equality with God
> as something to manipulate or exploit.

No, he chose to be emptied—
> to be obedient,
> to become like a slave,
> to become like us
> because he was born, like us:

Human.

This Jesus chose humility,
    became flesh and blood,
    and took on the vulnerability
    of being human,
    to the point and place of surrender—
    a deep and intentional surrender to the cross.

So,
    it is because of this
    that God lifted him high,
    naming him
    with the most blessed name,
    above any other.

So,
    at this name—
    this name, "Jesus,"
    all will be humbled as well,
    including everything in heaven,
    everything on earth,
    and everything below:
    kneeling, singing,
    proclaiming full-throated,
    to God's infinite glory:
    "Jesus Christ – is the Lord!"

And this witness and surrender of faith
    is pointed solely,
    and completely,
    to the glory of God.

(DH, adapt.)

Colossians 1:12-20

Firstborn in creation,
Firstborn from the dead—
Christ is our peace.

Give thanks!

Everyone—give thanks to God,
    who has made us all worthy and blessed,
    worthy and blessed to be connected,
    to be a part of a light-filled community,
    rescued from darkness,
    and led to be one
    with God's beloved,
    the Son—
    gifting us with the ultimate presence
    of mercy.

We cannot see God,
    but we can—and do—
    see and know,
    this Christ.

This Christ is God, walking with us.
This Christ is the firstborn of all creation.

The universe flourishes through Christ.
Everything that is seen and unseen,
    every form of power, strength, and authority
    springs forth from Christ,
    made real through and for Christ.

Christ was—before anything else
    could ever be dreamed of.

We survive
and are brought and held together
    by this most blessed Christ.

Christ is the guiding vision of the body,
    this fragile community called "church."
Beginning, firstborn of those passed,
    to be first among all.

God delights in this Christ
    and opens up the space
    for Christ to shine forth
    to the greatest fulfillment of glory,
    bringing all creation to God,
    and by making peace
    by his sacrifice;
    by his cross.

(DH, adapt.)

2 Timothy 1:5a, 6-9a

We accept God's most holy calling.

We remember your faith—
    most sincere...

And so,
    because of this
    we want to remind you
    to keep stirring into a flame
    this gift from God
    that is deep within you.

We are not cowards,
    for God's spirit

is one of power,
of love,
and of self-control.

So, knowing this,
we should not be ashamed at all
of testifying to this God of ours...

Join us, then,
in sharing this blessed hardship
with the strength and courage
that comes from God.

This God has saved us.

We are invited to accept
this most holy calling—
ignited by God's grace.

(DH, adapt.)

1 Peter 2:21-24

In Christ, our failings are crucified.
Through Christ, our wounds are healed.

Through and in Christ,
the state of our lives,
the flawed choices and consequences,
our very lives,
have been healed and restored.

Christ was and is blameless;
nothing untrue ever sounded from his mouth.

When attacked,
Christ never responded with revenge.
When tortured and taunted,

Christ never unleashed threats of harm in return
but gave himself over to the ultimate judge.

Christ carried in his very body
        all of our weakness and sin—
        all the way to a cross.

This was done
        so that we may join—
        in the midst of our death—
        a celebration of life proclaiming justice.

Christ's wounds became our healing.

They still are.

(DH, adapt.)

1 John 1:1-4

Christ is the Word of life.

We have always known this,
        from the beginning—
        we have heard it,
        we have seen it with our eyes,
        we have gazed upon it
        and touched it with our hands:

        The Word of life.
        Visible.

Again, know this:
        we have seen it
        and we give witness to it—
        it is true!

This gift of everlasting life
> that has always come from God
> was made real for us—
> this glorious truth
> we now proclaim and share with you,
> so that you can share
> in the community of love
> with us;
> because this connection with one another
> is with God
> and with the Christ.

We share this with all of you,
> so that our joy may be full and whole.

(DH, adapt.)

Revelation 19:1-7

> *All you servants of God—*
> *Sing praise, always!*

Sing Alleluia!
All that is good and powerful,
> bring it all to God's feet!
> God's judgments,
> God's decisions,
> are just and complete!
Alleluia!

Sing Alleluia!
All of you,
> everyone who holds a servant's heart,
> sing your praise!
Let your awe of God lift you up,
> and carry your praise!
Alleluia!

Sing Alleluia!
Why?
Because this God is in charge,
     and rules and guides us in all things!
So be filled
     with gladness, rejoicing,
     and relentless glory!
Alleluia!

Sing Alleluia!
The wedding feast,
     the great "bringing together,"
     now begins!
The bride is radiant in blinding beauty,
     in an amazing light-filled radiance of glory!
Alleluia! Alleluia!

(DH, adapt.)

Night Prayer

> Protect us God, as we are still awake;
> keep watch over us in our sleeping,
> so that while we are awake
> we may be attentive with Christ,
> and while we are asleep, rest in his peace.

(Saint Augustine, DH, adapt.)

GOSPEL CANTICLE

Luke 2:29-32

The Canticle of Simeon

> God, I am your servant.
> If I must die,
>> I can now make the journey
>> with complete surrender
>> on the wind of your peace,
>> as you promised.
>
> With my eyes—full of heart—
>> I have seen,
>> and see even more clearly now
>> the place of safety
>> that you have made ready
>> for all whom you hold close to your heart.

Revealing light.
Blazing glory.
A place among your people.
I belong to you.

(DH, adapt.)

(*Welcome, Faithful Presence*)

God,
thank you for the mystery of the night,
the home and holder of dreams.
Nourish the upcoming sleep
with stories of the depths of your love.
May the wonderful images that lie ahead
dream a new vision of your love.
Thank you for the gift of stars,
the brightness of the moon,
and all the sounds of night.

Help me not be fearful of night,
but embrace it as the center of peace.
May I hold the silence—
which is the best music of all—
because it is there
where some of the finest melodies are sung;
it is there where you dwell most clearly,
and where you call me most honestly
to live in faithfulness to you.

(DH, *With Every Note I Sing*)

Musical Suggestions

The following musical suggestions are compositions by David Haas and are all available from GIA Publications, Inc. What is listed here are the catalog numbers for the printed music editions. In addition to the musical resources listed below, much of this music is also included the various hymnal resources that are published by GIA Publications and other publishers. All of the titles below are also available from GIA as MP3 Digital Downloads and part of various CD recordings. The majority of the recorded versions of these compositions are also available on iTunes.

To contact GIA:
GIA Publications, Inc.
7404 South Mason Avenue
Chicago, IL 60638
1-800-442-1358
www.giamusic.com

For licensing information of David's music, contact:
ONE LICENSE
www.onelicense.net

MORNING PRAYER

Hymns and Songs

> God Is Alive (*From the collection, "Light and Peace"* G-3079)
> This Day God Gives Me (*G-3950*)
> You Are the Voice (*G-2705*)
> We Praise You (*G-5814*)
> Arise, Shine Out (*G-4868*)
> Alleluia, Sing! (*G-3583*)
> Stand Up, Friends (*G-3948*)
> God of All Creation (*G-3503*)
> Christ is Risen! Shout Hosanna! (*G-4870*)
> Alleluia! Our God Is Speaking (*G-7727*)
> Send Us Your Spirit (*G-3340*)
> God Is Here (*G-6687*)
> Throughout All Time (*G-4713*)
> Who Calls You By Name (*G-4865*)
> Join the Gospel Song (*G-8335*)
> Be A Blessing (*G-8857*)

Psalms and Canticles

Most of the psalm settings listed here are from the following four collections of the "Psalms for the Church Year" series, from GIA Publications:

* From Psalms for the Church Year, Vol. 1 (*G-2664*)

** From Psalms for the Church Year, Vol. 3 (*G-3325*)

*** From Psalms for the Church Year, Vol. 8 (*G-4579*)

**** From Psalms for the Church Year, Vol. 9 (*G-5041*)

All other psalm settings are available as separate choral editions or in other editions, and the catalog numbers are included below.

Also recommended are the many psalm settings composed by David and other composers in the series, "Cry Out With Joy" from GIA (*G-8480 / G-8481 / G-8482 / G-8483*).

Psalm 63: I Sing to You (*G-8967*)
Psalm 63: In the Shadow of Your Wings (*From the collection, "Light and Peace" G-3079*)
Psalm 51: Create In Me A Clean Heart *
Psalm 51: You Welcome in Me (*G-7721*)
Psalm 5: I Pray to You (*G-8334*)
Psalm 8: How Majestic Is Your Name (*G-8923*)
Psalm 8: Your Wonderful Name * * * *
Psalm 19: Lord. You Have the Words *
Psalm 19: The Ways of God (*G-6696*)
Psalm 19: The Stars Declare His Glory (*From the collection, "Light and Peace" G-3079*)
Psalm 19: Their Message Fills the World * * * *
Psalm 24: Reach Toward Heaven (*G-6161*)
Psalm 27: The Lord Is My Light *
Psalm 27: In the Land of the Living (*G-3448*)
Psalm 27: God Is My Light (*From the collection, "Light and Peace" G-3079*)
Psalm 29: The Lord Will Bless All People * * *
Psalm 36: The Fountain of All Life * * * * *
Psalm 41: O God, Heal My Soul * * *
Psalm 42: I Thirst for You (*G-4688*)
Psalm 57: I Will Wake up the Dawn (*G-8329*)
Psalm 65: The Seed that Falls * * *
Psalm 84: How Lovely * * * *
Psalm 86: Goodness and Forgiveness * * * *
Psalm 92: Lord, It Is Good (*G-4800*)
Psalm 95: If Today You Hear God's Voice *
Psalm 97: Our God Is Here * * * *
Psalm 98: All the Ends of the Earth *
Psalm 118: Alleluia! Let Us Rejoice * *

Psalm 118: This is the Day (*From the collection, "Walking by Faith" G-4831*)
Psalm 100: We Are God's People *
Psalm 100: God's People (*From the collection, "Walking by Faith" G-4831*)
Psalm 117: Go Out to All the World ***
Psalm 119: How I Love Your Commands ***
Psalm 119: Receive Me, God ****
Psalm 146: As Long As I Live ****
Psalm 148: Praise from the Heights ****
Psalm 150: Let All Creation Sing Praise (*G-8337*)
Psalm 150: Singing Praise to God ****

Canticle of Zachary (*Benedictus*):
  Blest Are You (*From the collection, "Walking by Faith" G-4831*)
Canticle of Zachary (*Benedictus*):
  Blest Be the God of Israel (*From the collection, "Light and Peace" G-3079*)
Canticle of Isaiah (*Is. 2:2–5*):
  Enter God's House (*G-7724*)
Canticle of Isaiah (*Is. 9:1–6*):
  Great Joy (*G-5210*)
Canticle of Ezekiel:
  You Make All Things New (*G-5181*)
Canticle of Sirach:
  Like the Sweet Fragrance (*From the collection, "Walking by Faith" G-4831*)

EVENING PRAYER

Hymns and Songs

> O Radiant Light (*From the collection, "We Have Been Told" G-2700*)
> At Evening (*From the collection, "Light and Peace" G-3079*)
> You Are Always Present (*G-7723*)
> All Is Brought to Life (*G-7735*)
> In the Power of Christ (*G-6159*)
> The God of Second Chances (*G-6688*)
> Abide, O Spirit of Life (*G-6691*)
> I Want to Call You (*G-3561*)
> Christ Among Us (*G-7165*)
> All I Want (*G-5190*)
> How Shall I Sing to God? (*G-3453*)

Psalms and Canticles

Most of the psalm settings listed here are from the following four collections of the "Psalms for the Church Year" series, from GIA Publications:

* From Psalms for the Church Year, Vol. 1 (*G-2664*)

** From Psalms for the Church Year, Vol. 3 (*G-3325*)

*** From Psalms for the Church Year, Vol. 8 (*G-4579*)

**** From Psalms for the Church Year, Vol. 9 (*G-5041*)

All other psalm settings are available as separate choral editions or in other editions, and the catalog numbers are included below.

Also recommended are the many psalm settings composed by David and other composers in the series, "Cry Out With Joy" from GIA (*G-8480 / G-8481 / G-8482 / G-8483*).

Psalm 141: My Prayers Rise Before You Like Incense
(*From the collection, "Light and Peace"G-3079*)

Psalm 15: Blest Are the Pure of Heart (*G-8856*)

Psalm 15: They Who Do Justice * *

Psalm 16: Only You (*G-6162*)

Psalm 16: Show Me the Path * * *

Psalm 16: The Path of Life
(*From the collection, "Who Calls You By Name, Vol. 1" G-3193*)

Psalm 27: I Will See How Good God Is (*G-8966*)

Psalm 27: God Is My Light (From the collection, "Light and Peace" *G-3079*)

Psalm 30: I Will Praise You, Lord * *

Psalm 32: God, I Confess My Wrong * * * *

Psalm 62: My Soul Waits for God (*G-7732*)

Psalm 62: In God Alone * *

Psalm 67: O God, May the Nations Praise You * * *

Psalm 72: In the Time of God (*G-5657*)

Psalm 112: A Light Shines (*G-5188*)

Psalm 113: Nations and Heavens * * *

Psalm 116: The Name of God * *

Psalm 121: God Is Ever Wakeful * * *

Psalm 121: The Mountain I See (*G-2925*)

Psalm 122: I Was Glad (*G-4143*)

Psalm 123: Our Eyes Rest on You (*G-9468*)

Psalm 124: Our Soul Has Escaped * * * *

Psalm 126: God Works Wonders * * *

Psalm 131: My Soul Is Still (*G-2924*)

Psalm 136: Everlasting Grace Is Yours * * *

Psalm 138: The Fragrance of Christ * *

Psalm 139: Before I Was Born (*G-5182*)

Psalm 139: You've Searched Me (*G-3501*)

Psalm 145: I Will Praise Your Name *

Psalm 145: I Will Bless You Every Day (*G-7918*)

Psalm 145: Faithful God * * * *

Psalm 145: We Are Led by the Hand of God ***
Psalm 147: Jerusalem, Give Glory (*G-9487*)

Canticle of Mary (*Magnificat*):
    Tell Out, My Soul (*From the collection, "Light and Peace" G-3079*)
Canticle of Mary (*Magnificat*):
    Magnificat (*G-3447*)
Canticle of Mary (*Magnificat*):
    Holy Is Your Name (*G-3334*)
Philippians Canticle:
    Jesus Christ Is Lord (*G-7728*)
Canticle of Peter:
    By His Wounds We Were Healed (*G-8328*)

MIDDAY PRAYER

Psalms

Most of the psalm settings listed here are from the following four collections of the "Psalms for the Church Year" series, from GIA Publications:

* From Psalms for the Church Year, Vol. 1 (G-2664)

** From Psalms for the Church Year, Vol. 3 (G-3325)

*** From Psalms for the Church Year, Vol. 8 (G-4579)

**** From Psalms for the Church Year, Vol. 9 (G-5041)

All other psalm settings are available as separate choral editions or in other editions, and the catalog numbers are included below.

Also recommended are the many psalm settings composed by David and other composers in the series, "Cry Out With Joy" from GIA (G-8480 / G-8481 / G-8482 / G-8483).

Psalm 23: You Are My Shepherd ****
Psalm 25: Remember Your Mercies **
Psalm 25: To You, O Lord ****
Psalm 34: The Goodness of God (G-3456)
Psalm 34: Come, My Children **
Psalm 104: Lord, Send Out Your Spirit *
Psalm 128: To Walk in God's Path ***

NIGHT PRAYER

Hymns and Songs

> God, Who Made the Earth and Heaven (*G-8338*)
> Compassion (*G-8965*)
> Steal Away (*G-4693*)
> Give Me Jesus (*G-5191*)

Psalms and Canticles

Most of the psalm settings listed here are from the following four collections of the "Psalms for the Church Year" series, from GIA Publications:

* From Psalms for the Church Year, Vol. 1 (*G-2664*)

** From Psalms for the Church Year, Vol. 3 (*G-3325*)

*** From Psalms for the Church Year, Vol. 8 (*G-4579*)

**** From Psalms for the Church Year, Vol. 9 (*G-5041*)

All other psalm settings are available as separate choral editions or in other editions, and the catalog numbers are included below.

Also recommended are the many psalm settings composed by David and other composers in the series, "Cry Out With Joy" from GIA (*G-8480 / G-8481 / G-8482 / G-8483*).

> Psalm 4: Enlighten Our Eyes (*From the collection, "Psalms for the Seasons" G-6181*)
> Psalm 91: Be With Me ****
> Psalm 103: Deep Down in My Soul (*G-3953*)
> Psalm 134: In the Silence of Night (*From "Psalms for the Church Year, Vol. 8" G-4579*)

Canticle of Simeon:
Now, O Lord, Dismiss Your Servants
(*From "Do This In Memory of Me" G-5433*)

PRAYERS OF GRATITUDE AND INTERCESSION

Morning Prayers (*From the collection, "Light and Peace" G-3079*)

Evening Intercessions (*From the collection, "Light and Peace" G-3079*)

Prayer of the Faithful (*From "Mass of Christ, Our Hope" G-7114*)

General Intercessions: If You Believe and I Believe (*From "Mass: Jesus the Compassion of God" G-4990*)

General Intercessions (*From "Mass for a New World" G-7803*)

General Intercessions (*From the collection, "Walking by Faith" G-4831*)

The Prayers: Remember Your Mercies (*From "Do This in Memory of Me" G-5433*)

God's Cause (*G-7670*)

Lord, the Work Is Yours (*G-8854*)

Also recommended are the many settings of the Universal Prayers composed by Lori True, from the series "Cry Out With Joy" from GIA (*G-8480 / G-8481 / G-8482 / G-8483*).

Seasonal Reflections

To listen to the Church
is to listen to the Lord of the Church.
Specifically,
this means taking part in the Church's liturgical life.
Advent, Christmas,
Lent, Easter,
Ascension and Pentecost:
These seasons and feasts teach you
to know Jesus better and better
and unite you more and more intimately
with the divine life he offers you in the Church.

(HN, *Letters to Marc About Jesus: Living a Spiritual Life in a Material World*)

ADVENT

To wait open-mindedly
is an enormously radical attitude toward life.
It is trusting that something will happen to us
that is far beyond our own imaginings.
It is giving up control over our future
and letting God define our life.
It is living with the conviction
that God molds us according to God's love
and not according to our fear.

(HN, *The Path of Waiting*; DH, adapt.)

We can really wait
only if what we are waiting for
has already begun for us.
So waiting is never a moment
from nothing to something.
It is always a movement
from something to something more.

(HN, *The Path of Waiting*)

CHRISTMAS

Songs, music, good feelings,
beautiful liturgies, nice presents,
big dinners, and many sweet words
do not make Christmas.
Christmas is saying "yes"
to something beyond all emotions and feelings.
Christmas is saying "yes" to a hope
based on God's initiative,
which has nothing to do
with what I think or feel.
Christmas is believing that the salvation of the world
is God's work and not mine.

(HN, *The Road to Daybreak: A Spiritual Journey*)

As soon as we call God,
"God-with-us,"
we enter into a new relationship of intimacy with him.
By calling him Emmanuel,
we recognize that he has committed himself
to live in solidarity with us,
to share our joys and pains,
to defend and protect us,
and to suffer all of life with us.
The God-with-us is a close God,
a God we call our refuge,
our stronghold, our wisdom,
and even, more intimately,
our helper, our shepherd, our love.

(HN, *Compassion: A Reflection on the Christian Life*;
DH, adapt.)

LENT

Lent is a time of returning to God.
It is a time to confess
how we keep looking for joy, peace, and satisfaction
in the many people and things surrounding us,
without really finding what we desire.
Only God can give us what we want.
So we must be reconciled with God,
as Paul says,
and let that reconciliation be the basis
of our relationship with others.
Lent is a time of refocusing,
of re-entering the place of truth,
of reclaiming our true identity.

(HN, *Sabbatical Journey*; DH, adapt.)

Certainly praying takes some admissions.
It requires the humble recognition
of our own condition as broken human beings.
However,
prayer does not lead us to shame, guilt, or despair,
but rather to the joyful discovery
that we are only human
and that God is truly God.

(HN, *With Open Hands*)

HOLY WEEK / TRIDUUM

PALM SUNDAY

Every time I look at this Christ on a donkey,
I am reminded again
that I am seen by him with all my sins,
guilt, and shame
and loved with all his forgiveness,
mercy and compassion.
(HN, The Road to Daybreak: A Spiritual Journey)

MONDAY

Through his death our death is transformed
from a totally absurd end of all
that gives life its meaning
into an event that liberates us
and those whom we love.

(HN, *A Letter of Consolation*)

TUESDAY

Jesus fulfills his mission not by what he does,
but by what is done to him....
It is good news to know
that Jesus is handed over to passion
and through his passion

accomplishes his divine task on earth.
It is good news for a world
passionately searching for wholeness.

(HN, *The Road to Daybreak: A Spiritual Journey*)

WEDNESDAY

This is the voice that Jesus wants us to hear.
It is the voice that calls us always
to return to the one
who has created us in love
and wants to re-create us in mercy.

(HN, *The Road to Daybreak: A Spiritual Journey*)

HOLY THURSDAY

Jesus does not want us to keep anything for ourselves.
Rather,
he wants our love to be as full,
as radical,
and as complete as his own.
He wants us to bend ourselves to the ground
and touch the places in each other
that most need washing.

(HN, *The Road to Daybreak: A Spiritual Journey*; DH, adapt.)

GOOD FRIDAY

Yes, it is a good Friday.
In the midst of all the grief and mourning,
there is sweet consolation.
We are together,
and there is love pouring out
from our broken hearts
and from the pierced heart of God.

(HN, *Sabbatical Journey*)

HOLY SATURDAY

Of all the days in history,
Holy Saturday—
the Saturday during which the body of Jesus
lay in the tomb in silence and darkness
behind the large stone
that was rolled against its entrance—
is the day of God's solitude.
It is the day on which the whole creation
waits in deep inner rest.
It is the day on which no words are spoken,
no proclamations made.
This Holy Saturday is the most quiet of all days ...
From this silence,
the Word will be spoken again and make all things
new.

(HN, *The Path of Waiting*)

EASTER

Jesus didn't rise from the grave
to baffle his opponents,
to make a victory statement,
or to prove to those who crucified him
that he was right after all.
Jesus rose as a sign to those who loved him
and followed him
that God's divine love is stronger than death.

(HN, *Bread for the Journey: Thoughts for Every Day of the Year*)

While many question
whether the resurrection really took place,
I wonder if it doesn't take place every day
if we have the eyes to see
and the ears to hear.

(HN, *Sabbatical Journey*)

PENTECOST

Each individual human being
can claim the Spirit of Jesus
as the guiding spirit of his or her life.
In that Spirit we can speak and act freely
and confidently with the knowledge
that the same Spirit that inspired Jesus
is inspiring us.

(HN, *Sabbatical Journey*)

The fruits of the Spirit of God -
joy, peace, patience, kindness, goodness,
trustfulness, gentleness, and self control -
cannot be limited to interpersonal relationships.
They have dimensions which far exceed
the small circles of friends, family, and community.
They carry in themselves
a worldwide dynamic that we call mission...

(HN, *In the House of the Lord: The Journey from Fear to Love*)

Blessings & Other Prayers

A spiritual life without prayer
is like the Gospel without Christ.

(HN, *The Only Necessary Thing: Living A Prayerful Life*)

Blessings

God of this meal and every meal,
we gather here at the table of your grace.
We come with all of our hungers,
aching for you to strengthen us,
to fill us,
and to sustain us.
Help us to eat, drink,
and share this food with grace,
and with gratitude and care.
May this food that we share,
and our words and laughter,
become a fest of love.
May your grace,
your love,
your life,
touch and embrace us. Amen.

(DH, *I Will Sing Forever* / *Meal Blessing*)

God,
we thank you for (name);
for his/her life;
for the journey of years
that have come to this moment.

We thank you for how he/she
has been a part of our lives,
for the good and fun times,
and for how he/she has made our lives better
for being with us.

Be with her/him today
to celebrate well
and to look forward
to many, many birthdays and good times ahead.

(DH, *To Give You A Future with Hope* / *Birthday Blessing*)

May God be with us,
now,
always as throughout all time.
May God never leave us,
never abandon us,
and never leave us orphaned.
Let our hearts be drawn to God,
and may our steps
follow God's steps.
May God's law
be kept by each and every one of us.
God led our parents in faith,
and they surrendered their lives to that faith.
So let us do the same.

(DH, *I Will Sing Forever* / *Inspired from 1 Kings 8:57–58*)

May our God,
who is the foundation of all patience
and encouragement,
enable us to live in perfect harmony with one
another
according to the spirit of Christ,
so that with full heart and voice
we may give glory to God.

May God,
who is the source of hope,
fill us with joy and peace,
so that through the power of the Holy Spirit
we may have unending hope.

May the God of peace be with all of us.

(DH, *With Every Note I Sing* / *Adapt. from Romans 15:5–6, 13, 33*)

We pray that God will pour out upon us
the many gifts which reflect God's promise.
May God strengthen us within,
and make a home in our hearts,
with justice and compassion at the center of our lives.
Then we will be able to fully understand
the unbelievable love of Christ,
and to know this love
which is beyond our comprehension,
so that we may walk with God.

(DH, *With Every Note I Sing / Adapt. from Ephesians 3:16–19*)

May the peace of God,
which is beyond our understanding,
keep watch over our hearts and minds
in Jesus Christ.
Finally, my friends,
all of our thoughts should be centered
on all that is true,
all that is worthy of respect,
all that is honest, pure, decent,
virtuous, or deserving of praise.
May we live
according to what we have learned.
Then the peace of God will be with us.

(DH, *With Every Note I Sing / Adapt. from Philippians 4:7–9*)

May God,
who is our peace,
bless us all completely;
may our spirits and souls
be kept pure and sound
when Jesus comes again.

(DH, *I Will Sing Forever / Adapt. from 1 Thessalonians 5:23*)

May these wonderful gifts from God:
mercy,
peace,
and love,
be ours in abundance.

(DH, *I Will Sing Forever* / *Adapt. from Jude 2*)

May the God of all grace,
who called us to everlasting glory in Christ,
restore, affirm, strengthen,
and establish all who know suffering.
Glory to God forever and ever.

(DH, *With Every Note I Sing* / *Adapt. from 1 Peter 5:10–11*)

May all things move and be moved in us.
May all things know and be known in us.
May all creation dance for joy within us.

(DH, *Adapted from the Chinook Psalter*)

Gospel kindred,
how I love thee;
tongue nor pen can never say
the very feelings of affection
growing stronger day by day.

Together we travel with the Gospel,
and we bow down to what is true,
and tell the world that Christ our Savior
is creating things anew.

(Adapt. DH, *With Every Note I Sing* / *Shaker Hymn*)

Teach me the songs of your truth, O Lord,
that I may bear fruit in you.
Open to me the music of your spirit,
that with every note I sing,
I may praise you.
Out of your kindness grant me this.
For you are the answer to all our needs.
Alleluia!

(DH, *With Every Note I Sing / Adapted from the Odes of Solomon, 2nd cent.*)

God,
Abba of all creation,
of the heavens and earth,
you are the source of the singing stars,
you are our loving parent.

We name and honor you for who you are—
Our God who is living,
and beyond our understanding.

May your future be our future,
May your promise be our destiny.

May your word be the ultimate word
in all our disputes;
may you reign in our lives today and every day.

We implore you to keep us safe,
sustain us with all that we may need
to live as you would have us live.

May the compassion and mercy

that we share with others
be the quality of the compassion
we find in you toward us.

Do not allow
the power of pain and suffering to destroy us;
do not test us beyond our own strength.

Keep us far away
from all that is in conflict with you;
all that is evil,
all that would isolate us from the gift of your love.

We await you,
we sing of the coming of your reign,
we dance to the music of your power,
and we share in the glory that comes from you
and surrounds us.

All this is yours.
Always.

(DH, *With Every Note I Sing / Inspired from the Lord's Prayer*)

Glory be to the Source of all things!
To Jesus the Christ!
To the Great Spirit!
From our beginnings
to the time beyond our death,
may light and life never end.

(DH, *With Every Note I Sing / Inspired from the Gloria Patri*)

You, Mary,
You are close to God.
You are blest and holy.
You are the bearer of the anointed One,

You are the human source of God walking with us.
        You are our Mother as well,
        and we cry for your prayer
        and investment in us when we falter.
        Be with us now,
        throughout all our days. Amen.

(DH, *With Every Note I Sing / Inspired from the "Hail Mary"*)

        Today, O Lord—I say YES to you!
        Today, O Lord—I say YES to life!
        Today, O Lord—I say YES to truth!
        Today, O Lord—I say YES to kindness!
        Today, O Lord—I say YES to gentleness!
        Today, O Lord—I say YES to honesty!
        Today, O Lord—I say YES to peace!
        Today, O Lord—I say YES to compassion!
        Today, O Lord—I say YES to community!
        Today, O Lord—I say YES to goodness!
        Today, O Lord—I say YES to beauty!
        Today, O Lord—I say YES to joy!
        Today, O Lord—I say YES to healing!
        Today, O Lord—I say YES to love!

(DH, *To Give You A Future With Hope*)

        I know and believe
        that you will laugh with me,
        cry with me,
        and walk lonely roads with me.

(DH, *Your Call is Constant*)

Indexes

PSALM-POEM INDEX

PSALM	PAGE
4	226
5	16
8	104, 210
11	19
15	19
16	57
19	69
20	26
21	26
23	215
24	22
25	216
27	33, 34
29	16
30	41, 72
32	41
33	23
34	217
36	29
41	48
42	68
43	75
45	71
46	49
47	30
48	38
49	78
51	44, 95, 149, 200
55	145
57	37
62	85
63	8
65	75
67	86, 130
71	218
72	91

73	92	117	52, 157
77	81	118	59, 163
80	88	119	51, 56, 156
81	89	120	79
84	120	121	100
85	128	122	160
86	136	123	125
87	142	124	126
88	227	125	133
90	170	126	139
91	229	127	140
92	102, 208	128	221
93	113	130	161
95	236	131	134
96	122	132	146
97	81	134	232
98	137	135	153, 154, 172
99	143	136	175, 176
100	45, 150	137	182
101	178	138	183
102	219	139	190, 191
103	230	141	4
104	220	142	5
108	186	143	194
110	13, 63, 117, 167	144	179, 197, 198
111	118	145	204, 205
112	168	146	187
113	110	147	96, 194, 201
114	14	148	114
115	64	149	10
116	99, 110	150	60, 164

CANTICLE INDEX

CANTICLE	PAGE
Exodus 15:1–18	243
1 Samuel: 2:1–10	245
1 Chronicles 29:10–13	247
Judith 16:2–3a, 13–15	248
Sirach 14:20; 15:3–a, 6b	248
Sirach 39:13–16a	249
Isaiah 2:2–5	250
Isaiah 9:1–2, 4–6	251
Isaiah 12:1–6	252
Isaiah 26:1–4, 7–9, 12	253
Jeremiah 14:17–21	254
Jeremiah 17:7–8	255
Lamentations 5:1–7, 15–17, 19–21	256
Ezekiel 26:24–28	257
Daniel 3:56–88	258
Daniel 12:2–3	260
Hosea 6:1–3, 6	260
Micah 4:5–7	261
Luke 1:46–55	264
Luke 1:68–79	241
Luke 2:29–32	234, 276
Ephesians 1:3–10	267
Philippians 2:5–11	268
Colossians 1:12–20	270
2 Timothy 1:5a, 6–9a	271
1 Peter 2:21–24	272
1 John 1:1–4	273
Revelation 19:1–7	274

Gratitude

Gratitude basically means
to receive the gifts of others—
to say thank you for being you.
It is a central part of ministry
to receive the gifts of others.

(HN, *"Parting Words"*)

I first want to express thanks to my dear friend Jim Knipper of Clear Faith Publishing, for his friendship, generosity, and lavish support of all my creative efforts; and for his true spirit of "Diakonia." Thanks also to Jan Richardson for her amazing visual images; to Maureen Edore at Clear Faith, and to Doug Cordes for his design work. I also want to send out a loud song of thanksgiving to Kathleen Hollenbeck for her tremendous and amazing work in editing this manuscript.

I'd like to express my deep gratitude to Robert Jonas, Michael Christiansen, Rebecca Laird, Fr. Ron Rohlheiser, OMI; and Sr. Sue Mosteller, CSJ; all from whom, by their relationship with Henri and their insight into his lens of the spiritual life, I have learned so much. Their wisdom has helped to provide a framework for this project.

A special word of thanks goes to my good friend Fr. Michael Joncas. His knowledge, love, and passion for the Liturgy of the Hours provided my earliest experiences with daily prayer. For that gift—and for so many other reasons—I give thanks to God for Michael and will always be very, very grateful indeed. I add to his name those who have been dear friends, guides, and partners in ministry over the years: Bonnie Faber, Art Zannoni, Lori True, Stephen Pishner, Stephen Petrunak, Joe Camacho, Jo Infante, Betsey Beckman, Fr. Ray East, Marty Haugen, Fr. James Bessert, Lou Anne Tighe, Bill Huebsch, Sr. Kathleen Storms, SSND; Fr. George DeCosta, Rob and Mary Glover, Mary Werner, Sr. Gertrude Foley, SC; Fr. Joe Kemp, Tom Franzak, Bishop Remi De Roo, Pearl Gervais, Zack Stachowski, Jes Garceau, Matt Reichert, and Kate Cuddy.

God bless Karen Pascal and the tremendous work of the Henri Nouwen Society (www.henrinouwen.org), for keeping Henri's legacy vibrant and generative for people throughout the world. I also want to send blessings out to Alec Harris and the entire family at GIA Publications in Chicago, who have been the outlet and home of safe-keeping for my song prayers over the years.

I express my deepest gratitude to many good and dear friends, colleagues, heroes, and spiritual guides—who together with those already mentioned, are witnesses and relentless "living reminders" of what it means to serve the Body of Christ: Alissa Hetzner, Fr. Alapaki Kim, Leisa Anslinger, Sr. Edith Prendergast, RC; Fr. Raymond Kemp, Andrea Goodrich, Sr. Paula Damiano, SP; Sr. Jan Craven, SP; Megan McKenna, Sr. Roxanne Seifert, PBVM; Fr. Bill Taylor, Kathy and Glenn Baybayan, Barbara Conley-Waldmiller, Br. Dennis Schmitz, SM; Jim Waldo, Fr. Bob DeLand, Rory Cooney, Stephen Petrunak, Sr. Helen Prejean, CSJ; Lisa Cressy, Sr. Jo Gaugier, OP; Anna Betancourt, Matt Maus, Sr. Andrea Lee, IHM; Thom Morris, Bro. Mickey McGrath, OSFS; Gary Daigle, Fr. Ricky Manalo, CSP; Lisa Habeck, Jaime Cortez, Joel Loecken, Fr. John Forliti, Pam Cole, and George Miller. It is impossible for me to not call to mind those dear friends and guides who have shaped my life and ministry so deeply over the years, and who now are feasting at the table of glory and grace: Sr. Roberta Kolasa, SJ; Sue Seid-Martin, Fr. Jim Dunning, Zola Rudd Patrick, Bishop Kenneth Untener, Leon Roberts, Ralph Kiefer, Fr. Eugene Walsh, SS; Mike Hay, and Derek Campbell. I never stop thanking God for all of you.

Finally, as always...there are no words to adequately express my love and gratitude to Jeffrey, Colleen, Mary, and Helen.

Oh ... how can I forget? Thank you, Henri.

Soli Deo Gloria!

DH

Sources

ABOUT THE AUTHOR

David Haas is from Eagan, Minnesota, where he is the director of The Emmaus Center for Music, Prayer and Ministry, in addition to serving as the animator for the Taize' Prayer Community at Cretin-Derham Hall in St. Paul, Minnesota. Highly regarded as one of the preeminent composers of liturgical music in the English-speaking world, he has produced and published over fifty collections and recordings with GIA Publications, and his music has been translated into many languages, appearing in hymnals of various Christian denominations through the world. Among his many popular song-prayers are *Blest Are They*, *You Are Mine*, *We Are Called*, *We Have Been Told*, *Song of the Body of Christ*, *The Name of God*, *Now We Remain*, *Who Calls You By Name*, *Prayer for Peace*, *Deep Within*, *Magnificat*, *The God of Second Chances*, and *Without Seeing You*, just to name a few.

David is the founder and executive director for *Music Ministry Alive!*, an international liturgical music formation institute for high school and college-age youth (www.musicministryalive.com) and has travelled extensively as a workshop presenter, conference speaker, and concert performer in all fifty states, as well as in Canada, Australia, The Bahamas, England, Ireland, Germany, Italy, Israel, Greece, Turkey, New Zealand, and Asia. A collector of icons, he is also the author of over thirty books in the areas of liturgy and music, prayer and spirituality, religious education, and youth ministry. In 2015, David was the recipient of an Honorary Doctorate in Humane Letters from the University of Portland in Oregon.

To order printed and recorded editions of David's many liturgical compositions, contact:
GIA Publications, Inc.
7404 South Mason Avenue
Chicago, IL 60638
1-800-442-1358
www.giamusic.com

For licensing information of David's music, contact:
ONE LICENSE
www.onelicense.net
1-800-ONE-1501

Gospel Canticle for Evening Prayer
Luke 1: 46-55 (DH, adapt.)
The Canticle of Mary (Magnificat)

My soul is bursting with how great God is!
My spirit cannot stop rejoicing,
    and I cannot begin to hold and take in
    the liberating power of God.

Why?

Because God's favor rests on me,
    in and out of, and because of my brokenness,
    in my feeble attempts to serve.

Beginning today,
    right here and right now,
    and with every day that will follow,
      and because God alone determines who I am,
    God's name for me – "the beloved"
    will keep ringing in my heart.

Relentless.

God has, and continues to do,
    amazing and spectacular things for me.
Holy things.
    "Holy is God" will be my constant song.

For all who revere and honor God,
    mercy is, and will be, given lavishly.
God's strength is beyond any hope I have,
    freeing me from the tyranny of self.

If I sit too high –
> if I put too much faith in my own power,
> God will shake my false towers to their
> foundation.

If I find myself drowning in quicksand,
> I will be lifted up to a higher,
> and a more glorious place.

When I hunger and ache,
> I will be filled and healed.
When I am too comfortable and secure,
> in and through things that are shallow,
> my comfort will become afflicted.
Then, redirected.
Restored.

When I am faithful, I am protected.
Mercy is lavishly given,
> promises are honored and kept.

I am God's beloved child.
I will never be forgotten.

(*Welcome, Faithful Presence*)

65779433R00194

Made in the USA
Middletown, DE
03 March 2018